THE SABBATH JOURNAL OF
JUDITH LOMAX
(1774–1828)

AMERICAN ACADEMY OF RELIGION
TEXTS AND TRANSLATIONS SERIES

Edited by

Terry Godlove
Hofstra University

Number 25
THE SABBATH JOURNAL OF
JUDITH LOMAX
(1774–1828)

Edited by
Laura Hobgood-Oster

The Sabbath Journal of Judith Lomax
(1774–1828)

Edited by
Laura Hobgood-Oster

Scholars Press
Atlanta, Georgia

THE SABBATH JOURNAL OF JUDITH LOMAX
(1774–1828)

Edited by
LAURA HOBGOOD-OSTER

Library of Congress Cataloging in Publication Data
Lomax, Judith, 1774–1828.
    The Sabbath journal of Judith Lomax, 1774–1828 / edited by Laura
Hobgood-Oster.
        p.   cm. — (American Academy of Religion. Texts and
translations series ; no. 25)
    Includes bibliographical references and index.
    ISBN 0-7885-0538-6 (pbk. : alk. paper)
    1. Lomax, Judith, 1774–1828—Diaries. 2. Episcopalian women—
Virginia—Diaries. 3. Women mystics—Virginia—Diaries.
4. Episcopalians—Virginia—Diaries. 5. Mystics—Virginia—Diaries.
I. Hobgood-Oster, Laura, 1964–   II. Title. III. Series: Texts and
translations series (American Academy of Religion) ; no. 25.
BX6093.L66A3   1999
283'.092—dc21
[b]   99-17812
                           CIP

Printed in the United States of America
on acid-free paper

*For my family
and
Judith*

Table of Contents

Acknowledgments

The voice of Judith Lomax remained silenced for too long. Hers is a contribution to the history of women in American religion that would have been recognized—had she been born male. The beauty of her prose, the fluidity of her poetry, the depth of her theological reflection, the desire of her heart to preach in a world that would not allow her to do so, and the intimate love she experienced with her God led to a passionate and vibrant theological, autobiographical work. Its insight will prove significant for those in historical, religious, women's, theological and American studies. Discovering these gifted women provides both joy and pain. The joy of delving into a fascinating life and providing that information for others is accompanied by the pain of realizing that her life may have been even more rewarding had she been allowed to develop her gifts to the utmost of her ability. As one hears her words, the deep sorrow of dreams unfulfilled—visions of leadership in evangelical Christianity, not permitted to a woman—becomes apparent. Still, the value of presenting her wisdom and the story of her life awaits affirmation.

A special note of thanks must be given to the Virginia Historical Society for preserving this and other incredible resources, many just waiting eagerly to be revealed. American Academy of Religion, Scholars Press and Dr. Terry Godlove, editor of the Texts and Translations Series, gave me the opportunity to present this piece for publication, hopefully their excitement about its possibilities will be captured by others. Also, to my colleagues in the Department of Religion and Philosophy at Southwestern University who, even if they do not know so, have patiently put up with the final touches of completing this publication.

I shall remain thankful for all of my days to my parents who have helped in the hands-on research, my siblings and my husband Jack, who scouted out Judith Lomax's old home and gravesite, among many other tasks. All of these supporters remain faithful even as I labor through seemingly endless academic projects. Of course, the most constant companions of all, our dog buddies—Beaugart and Cezar—wait for their much needed walks as I write away, thus they deserve the depths of my gratitude.

Dr. Laura Hobgood-Oster
Southwestern University
Georgetown, Texas
December 1998

Introduction

"The Lovely Visions of My Mind"

*...but I shrink from the World, for it is too often selfish, and unfeeling and
too often ready to throw the imputation of Enthusiasm, or romance on all
feelings as do not assimilate with its own.—but I trust those regions which
I love to contemplate, in that heaven to which I lift my hopes, that there
are some better modifications for these things—and oh, methinks I would
not for all the treasures of this world, relinquish these, the lovely visions
of my mind! and which I hope will one day be realized in heaven.*[1]

Judith Lomax was born into a world of emerging evangelical fervor and
tightly prescribed, though transforming, gender roles. A single woman who
lived in Virginia's Rappahannock River towns of Port Royal and
Fredericksburg, she molded a life from her own unique vision of evangelical
Christian faith and the strength it instilled within her. A record of her experience
as an independent woman in the midst of a patriarchal religious and social
culture survives in the form of a devotional journal, the extant portion of which
covers her mature years, from 1819-1827. The journal reflects the formation of
personal subjectivity which had burgeoned from both her personal and
communal religious experience.[2] It includes reflections on sermons, accounts of
worship rituals and events, tales of life among her circle of evangelical
companions, fascinating and theologically dense religious and liturgical poetry,
and intimate devotional meditations. She was witty, thoughtful and persistent,
living out her life as an individual bereft of traditional earthly attachments and

---

[1]Lomax, [November 1, 1821].

[2]I indicate "extant" here only because of her ability to write and her devotion to the
practice. Though there is no direct evidence of earlier journals, it is almost unimaginable that
she did not engage in this practice earlier in her life. The collection of poetry which she
published a decade prior to beginning this journal indicates that she spent much time in
reflective and creative writing. There seems little hope, however, of recovering any earlier
pieces.

support, yet bolstered by her complete devotion to evangelical Christianity and, more centrally, to her "Heavenly Bridegroom."

In and of itself, this historical and theological piece provides an irreplaceable window through which to view the life of a devout evangelical woman in the antebellum South. In this particularity one finds fertile fields of insight to plow, uncovering a wealth of wisdom rarely attributed to women of the era. Of course, a window to the overall ethos of the evangelical South also opens, though definitely through the perspective of one "who seeks after holiness, who longs to be perfected, longs for complete sanctification, and who thinks her heart's desire is with God." Such sources are inaccessible unless one has days or weeks to spend probing through various manuscript collections. Yet the knowledge which can be gained through studying these primary accounts of experiential religion proves priceless.

The introduction to Judith Lomax's journal will address several aspects having to do with her perspective and historical setting. First, what kind of journal did Lomax write? A specific, new sub-genre will be suggested—the Sabbath journal. Second, who was the "authoress," a term with which she described herself? A brief biography of her life will be outlined. Third and obviously connected to the first two questions, why does this particular journal warrant scholarly attention and publication for a broader audience? The answer to this question becomes apparent as one reads the text itself, but suggestions are offered. And, finally, what unique insights about women and religion in the "Old South" can be gleaned from this piece? One particular phenomenon, love mysticism, emerges as exceptionally provocative.

The audience for this piece should prove quite broad. For scholars in the fields of history, theology, religious studies, American studies and women's studies, the contribution seems all too obvious. In each of these related disciplines, there remains a dearth of primary source material penned by women. But, there is also appeal for the reader who is simply fascinated by the powerful story of the life of another seemingly "ordinary" person who proves to be extraordinary even as she remains hidden from the pages of standard histories and theological treatises. These "every people" demonstrate the most significant experiences of all as will be evident in the perusal of the interiority of Judith Lomax. Her seemingly mundane existence reveals all that is sacred in the lives of those regarded as less than prestigious–ones so rarely recalled.

That Link of Love Between My Heavenly Parent and Myself
The Genre of the Sabbath Journal

I cannot feel satisfied without a book of record between me and my God—
A book bound to the inmost recesses of my heart, where, I feel, as I do,
when bowed before the mercy seat, encompassed within the vail, where
none but God is nigh, and truth alone...[3]

The literary genre of the journal held a central position in the religious lives of evangelicals in the early nineteenth century, particularly in the spiritual lives of evangelical women.[4] Journals, or diaries, provided a devotional setting through which they related to God and in which they examined their own circumstances along with those of the world around them. These primary sources, revealing the words of women themselves rather than a secondary reporting most often written by men observing them, provide a rarely viewed glimpse into the religious lives of these women.

It has been suggested that the journal, in this case also a form of women's autobiography, arose directly from the genre of religious confession. Protestantism's focus on the individual struggle for salvation and the individual's relationship with God accentuated such confession, a poignant and affecting attribute of evangelical Christianity. The journal, as autobiography, claims "truth value"; the writer "purports to believe what s/he asserts."[5] William

---

[3]Caroline Homassel Thornton, Diary, May 24, 1841 (Virginia Historical Society, Richmond, Virginia).

[4]Evangelicalism ultimately cannot be defined, rather it must be understood as a process within history. In his work *Evangelicals and Conservatives in the Early South, 1740-1861* (Columbia: University of South Carolina Press, 1988) Robert Calhoon provides a description which proves helpful in clarifying this theological and practical strand within Christianity: "Evangelical Christianity is the proclamation of salvation through faith in Christ. It emphasizes the atonement for human sins through Christ's crucifixion, relies on Scriptural authority, and affirms the victory of God's grace over His law. As such, evangelical Christianity is a religious belief shared by converts and observable by those inside and outside the faith." (1) Central to an understanding of evangelicalism is the concept of "conversion," which will be illuminated further as it relates to Judith Lomax and the development of her gender subjectivity within the context of southern evangelicalism.

[5]Elizabeth Bruss, *Autobiographical Acts: The Changing Situation of a Literary Genre* (Baltimore: Johns Hopkins University Press, 1967), 10. For further information on the genre of women's autobiography the reader is directed to: Susan Stanford Friedman, "Women's Autobiographical Selves: Theory and Practice," in *The Private Self: Theory and Practice of*

Andrews, editor of a collection of autobiographies written by nineteenth-century African-American women, notes that journals chronicle the "realization of one's true place and destiny in the divine scheme of things" and "confront the problem of what [the diarist's] role should be as Christian women in the earthly realm."[6] The historical and theological background to the activity of religious journal composition proves fascinating and provides insight into a variety of examples of individual's religious conversion, construction and experience.[7]

Antebellum women's journals and diaries remain buried in manuscript collections throughout the South. Unlike the religious journals of women in New England or women within the Society of Friends, those of women in the South have not, to a significant degree, been the subject of historical or theological research.[8] Yet they contain myriad pieces of information pertinent to historical and theological study, particularly that which focuses on gender construction, its religious and cultural implications.[9]

Women's Autobiographical Writings, ed. S. Benstock (London: Routledge, 1988), 39-61. Felicity Nussbaum, *The Autobiographical Subject: Gender and Ideology in Eighteenth-Century England* (Baltimore: Johns Hopkins University Press, 1989); and Sidonie Smith, *A Poetics of Women's Autobiography* (Bloomington: Indiana University Press, 1987).

[6]William Andrews, *Sisters of the Spirit: Three Black Women's Autobiographies of the Nineteenth Century* (Bloomington: Indiana University Press, 1986), 11.

[7]This history is too lengthy for coverage in the introduction. Please see: Laura Hobgood-Oster, "Anticipating the Rich Gospel Feast," diss., St. Louis University, 1997, chapter five; Estelle Jelinek, *The Tradition of Women's Autobiography: From Antiquity to the Present* (Boston: Twayne, 1986); Metta L. Winter, "Heart Watching through Journal Keeping: A Look at Quaker Diaries and Their Uses," *Women's Diaries: A Quarterly Newsletter* 1:2 (Summer 1983): 1-3; Susan Starr Sered, "Conversations with Rabbanit Zohara: An Exploration of Gender and Religious Autobiography," *Journal of the American Academy of Religion* LXIII:2 (Summer 1995): 249-268.

[8]For recent research on diaries of women in New England see Karen V. Hansen, *'A Very Social Time': Crafting Community in Antebellum New England* (University of California Press, 1994). In this systematic study, she concludes that, among the antebellum diaries which she compared in New England, 46% of women recorded comments on religious services in their diaries, whereas only 17% of men did so. Likewise, 36% of women recorded theological reflections in diaries and, again, 17% of men did so.

[9]The exclusion of women's journals, in general, from publication and as subjects of scholarly research is evident in figures which note that for the period of 1629-1861 approximately 2,300 diaries were published in America. Of those 2,100 were by men and 165 were by women. Another bibliography lists the years of the "Early Republic," 1775-1827,

Within these journals some women list daily activities, offer information regarding family relationships, define financial matters and describe educational processes. Occasionally though, the journals are specifically devoted to religious reflection, thus constituting a subset of the genre. Though the journals vary in content, frequency and form, certain women devote themselves to the diligent practice, or as I contend religious ritual, of recording the events of the Sabbath in these journals.[10] Other reflections are also incorporated, but the spoke around which the wheel of these writings turns is most often the Sabbath. Intriguing commentaries regarding preachers and the spoken Word or sermon, fabulous worship experiences, enlightening descriptions of those members of the congregation present for worship, accounts of church social interaction, and the increasingly significant role of the Sabbath school are included. In addition, theological discourses regarding the nature of God, the essence of humanity, women's position in relationship to God, the nature of the world and soteriological reflections fill the journals. The complex theological issues which the women address point to minds engaging issues far beyond those of the purely domestic realm to which they were so often relegated by society.

Though they usually relate an account of the activities of the day, the primary journals with which I have dealt highlight the event of sharing the "Gospel feast," the performance and reception of preaching. Often, specific biblical texts are listed along with the preacher's name. They record reflections on and reactions to the Word preached, along with a praise or an occasional critique of the event. For this reason, I designate this sub-genre the "Sabbath journal." Judith Lomax's journal is the most fascinating, intellectually complex and aesthetically captivating example of the genre, which I have yet encountered.

---

and shows 1,354 men's diaries published as opposed to only 90 for women. See William Matthews, *American Diaries: An Annotated Bibliography of American Diaries Written Prior to the Year 1861* (Berkeley: University of California Press, 1945); Laura Arksey, Nancy Pries and Marcia Reed, *American Diaries Written from 1492 to 1844* (Detroit: Gale Research, 1983).

[10]Ritual can be defined variously: phenomenologically, practically, religiously, culturally, personally and communally. Mary Douglas, in *Natural Symbols* (New York: Random House, 1973), defines ritual as "preeminently a form of communication composed of culturally normal acts that have become distinctive by being diverted to special functions where they are given magical efficacy." (41, 97, 178) As will become evident as the journal of Lomax is explicated and reveals itself, such was the case.

In addition to being simply a method of keeping information about the Sabbath, or writing a traditional introspective and reflective spiritual diary, these Sabbath journals provided an opportunity for women to enter into discourse with their God, thus functioning as the aforementioned religious ritual performance for and by some evangelical women. While offering the historian an irreplaceable insight into general historical information about evangelicalism and about gender formation within a certain part of the community, they provide the theologian with an astonishing image of the personal relationship established between women and their understanding of the divine.

Sabbath journals, then, constitute ritual communications on several levels. Primarily they form a link of discourse between women and the divine, distinctive from the genre of journal which focused on record-keeping or purely personal introspection. In this sense Sabbath journals become "magical," or religiously significant. In addition, they communicate the recreated subjectivity of women as "heirs of immortality" and "spouse of God," two phrases often employed within the journals I have studied.

Within the leaves of these rich journals lies a wealth of substantive theological reflection, a commentary on everything religious and an insight into the communion with God or mystical union which, based upon the evidence in some fascinating journals mentioned herein, some antebellum evangelical women experienced. Such intimate religious phenomena cannot be uncovered in other forms, only through the words of individuals themselves—words preserved in these manuscripts.

The journals which I study sometimes take the form of prayer, other times of poetry, sometimes of dialogue and yet other times of joyful exclamation as women pondered God, themselves, the "world" and the religious society surrounding them. Their theological and historical richness must underlie any substantive study of evangelicalism as a whole in the antebellum South, particularly its pervading influence in the lives of devout women. As emphasized by Susan Starr Sered in her studies of more recent religious autobiography, women's autobiographical works, which include such journals, are "based upon (although not limited to) 'a group consciousness'—an awareness of the meaning of the cultural category WOMAN."[11] As autobiography, Sabbath journals reflect evangelical women's perception of themselves not only in relationship to God, but as gendered people constructed by evangelical society.

---

[11]Susan Starr Sered, 262.

The Life of Judith Lomax

Yes, yes, I feel the vital force, Of those rich streams that cleanse the heart
They flow with purifying course, Before them all my doubts depart.
For if in Christ I do believe, If him I love, then I am sav'd,
God's holy word can ne'er deceive, That giv'n, is on my heart Engrav'd
Let persecutions, or distress, Or ev'ry earth-born care annoy;
They ne'er can make my comforts less, If I the love of Christ enjoy.[12]

Born just before the Revolutionary War in the colony of Virginia, Judith Lomax would spend her life as a woman independent of attachments and support in a culture which stressed a woman's utter dependency. In this patriarchal culture, Judith Lomax survived, and at times even thrived, bolstered by her complete devotion to evangelical Christianity and her Heavenly Bridegroom.

Thomas and Anne Corbin Tayloe Lomax lived at Port Tobago, Caroline County, Virginia.[13] The Rappahannock River towns of Fredericksburg and Port Royal were surrounded by farming communities in this, one of the oldest sections of the English colonies. A confluence of rivers, the Chesapeake Bay and the nearby Atlantic ocean created both economies of trade and of agriculture. Nestled between Williamsburg, Richmond, Washington City and Baltimore, the area was simultaneously rural, but closely and easily connected to the centers of economic and political life in the era of the early Republic.

Judith Lomax, born September 25, 1774, was the first of twelve children born to Thomas and Anne. Many of the Lomax children survived into adulthood, and the family ties would simultaneously prove supportive and destructive for their eldest daughter throughout the course of her life. According to the will of Thomas Lomax, a tract of land "containing six hundred acres more or less" was left to his family. Hence, they were people of some economic means.

They were also people with familial connections. The Tayloe family was prominent in Virginia and in Washington City. John Tayloe, Judith Lomax's maternal uncle, served as a colonel in the military and lived in the midst of

---

[12]Lomax, "Devotional Stanzas."

[13]"Port Tobago" was also spelled "Portabago." It did not appear on contemporary maps, though it was in the same county as Port Royal. References to it by the Lomax family point to that being the name of their land specifically rather than the name of a town.

powerful Washington society. During the early years of the nineteenth-century Washington became the center of much of America's newly forming cultural milieu. Famous dignitaries visited and the city plan, founded on impressing these ambassadors, took shape. It was a city of power in a newly formed nation of democracy. The Lomax and Tayloe families were welcomed in this rapidly growing upper echelon of society.

In addition, Judith's brother, John Tayloe Lomax, studied law at St. John's College in Annapolis, Maryland and became the first professor of law at the University of Virginia.[14] Well known among both politicians and academics, this male sibling, who became the patriarch of the family following the death of Judith Lomax's father, wielded influence within wider society as well as within his immediate family. John Lomax completed his career as a circuit court judge in Fredericksburg, Virginia. The complex relationship between Judith Lomax and her brother John impacted her life greatly, both emotionally and financially.

Having prefaced the account of Judith Lomax's life with this outline of her family's social, political and economic status, it must be noted that she claimed to place no value on worldly possessions or rank. She accumulated no wealth, living on the edge of poverty throughout the years of her journaling and dying in the home of her mother since her dire financial straits caused her to leave her own small abode in Port Royal. Indeed, as she grew into an independent woman, after the death of her father, most of her earthly attachments to her blood relatives were severed in favor of those relationships she developed in the evangelical community.

Though little else is known detailing the years of her life prior to the surviving Sabbath journal, evidence does show that she endured tragedy and critical times of alienation from her family. Beginning in 1805 with the early death of her brother, Thomas, and the death of her father in 1811, the family experienced intense discord. Thomas Lomax divided the family property at Port Tobago between his sons, Thomas, John, Ralph, Mann and Edward.[15] There were also provisions in his will to care for his "loving wife" and funds "reserved

---

[14]John Tayloe Lomax also authored a three-volume *Digest of the Laws Respecting Real Property* and a two-volume *Treatise on the Law of Executors and Administrators* (1841). The most complete background on the Lomax family is Edward L. Lomax, *Genealogy of the Virginia Family of Lomax* (Chicago, 1913).

[15]The eldest son, Thomas, died in 1805, the third son, Ralph, died in 1814; the youngest son, Edward, died in 1818; Mann Page had relocated to South Carolina.

for the benefit of all my daughters," Judith, Rebecca, Catherine, Elizabeth, Marion, Eleanor and Sarah.[16] From this point forward, though, Judith Lomax's financial means were quite limited and her relationship with the male members of her family strained.

According to a letter which she sent to her aunt, Mrs. Washington of Haywood, in December 1815, male and female members of the Lomax family were alienated. The issue hinged around the sale of the family land, possibly as a result of overdue debts due on their father's land.[17] So with "bitter agony," Judith Lomax "tore [her]self away from dear Port Tobago." Indicating that she "should have staid until the last," she was forced to leave her "Mamma and Sisters" in a "trying hour."

From there she relocated to Port Royal, temporarily secured a room in her aunt's home and attempted to locate a place "where there are houses for Female Boarders." The entire episode appeared to her "like frightful dreams, or some tragic tale of woe that I have been reading." All of the female members of the family were "badly off." The executors of their father's estate held it in their discretion to dispense the "proportionable part of the paternal estate." When Judith Lomax left for Port Royal she had "from the estate" only "some Pork and meal."

Though all of the circumstances cannot be uncovered, one passage in the letter captured the distressing state in which Judith Lomax was situated:

> But think not that I have *willingly* left my Mother,—no, God who knows my heart, knows that *Nature* struggled *there*, and that I still wish'd to linger near her, but it cannot be, all wise Providence whose dispensations are unsearchable had decreed it otherwise, I *must* separate from my family, *there is no help for it*.—My Mother and my sisters are to reside at Menokin, where *I know* I am neither *desired* or *expected*...[18]

---

[16]"Will of Thomas Lomax of Caroline County, Virginia," testified April 26, 179[6], *Copies of Extant Wills*, Virginia Historical Society, 656-657.

[17]A suit, "Bernard vs. Lomax," was instigated in 1815. It listed outstanding debts, payable by sale of portions of the family property. Apparently the family, distressed by this entire episode, disintegrated.

[18]Letter from Judith Lomax to Mrs. Washington, December 28, 1815, Tayloe Family Papers, Mss1P2775a72, Virginia Historical Society.

In terms of her personal circumstances, the next indication appeared in a second letter addressed to her maternal uncle, Colonel John Tayloe, in 1819. By this time all of her brothers, with the exception of John Tayloe Lomax, had died. During the intermediate years she had purchased her "own little dwelling ... intirely out of *my own little independant* property, without soliciting one Cent from my Paternal estate..." In addition, she sent power of attorney to her uncle to draw a "Dividend from the Farmer's Bank of Alexandria" from "26 shares of Stock."[19] There was no direct indication regarding the source of her income, though it may have been from a book she published.

This book, published in Richmond in 1813, provides another fascinating piece of evidence from the years prior to the extant Sabbath journal. *The Notes of an American Lyre*, composed by Judith Lomax, contained a collection of poems.[20] The preface was a poem that described beautifully the understanding of gender of the "Authoress":

> STRANGE! That a timid Female, borne on Fancy's wing, should dare to soar a lot to the Muses!—But no, the little productions of my pen deserve not to be dignified with the title of Poetry; they are only the little effusions of a guileless heart...

The work contains poetry similar in style to that included in her journal. She composed lines dedicated to religion and others revelatory of her understanding of the nature of women:

> A Monitor, which I have, caused me last night to meditate on Female Vanity, and sleep had no sooner closed my eyes, than that busy dame Fancy, presented

---

[19]Letter from Judith Lomax to Col. John Tayloe, Washington City, District of Columbia, 16 March 1819, Tayloe Family Papers, MSS1P277a 73, Virginia Historical Society.

[20]Judith Lomax, *The Notes of an American Lyre* (Richmond: Samuel Pleasant, Near the Market Bridge, 1813). This is the only surviving copy which I have been able to locate and I assume the print run was not large. Interestingly, Judith Lomax was included in F.V. N. Painter's work *Poets of Virginia* (Richmond: B.F. Johnson, 1907) under the heading "The Period of the Revolution." Painter referred to her as the "fair authoress" who "beautifully illustrates the delicate culture of that good old time before the 'new woman' was dreamed of, or the gentle housewife ventured upon a thought beyond the sweet domestic sphere." (55-57) Obviously, Painter knew little of Judith Lomax and never fathomed how far beyond the domestic sphere, into the divine sphere, she traveled through the influence of, among other factors, evangelical Christianity.

to my view a young Female: She was arrayed in the becoming Robe of Native Simplicity and Virtue, and neatness were the ornaments which adorned her. Pensive she approached, and with modest air repeated to me the following lines:

> The Roses bloom and bloom but to decay;
> Such is our life,—and transitory day!
> At first in beauty's pride, we gay appear,
> And softly pass through each revolving year;
> But soon, alas! I say it with a sigh,
> Soon beauty fades,—too soon its colours fly.
> But graced with virtue, we may still be great,
> And smile defiance at the shafts of Fate;
> Then shall true taste in us, still beauties find,
> And hail the triumphs of a cultur'd Mind.[21]

A "cultured mind" proved of more lasting worth than a beauty's pride, which would "decay as the rose." Judith Lomax's talents for writing emerged even before she began to pen the one Sabbath journal which survived, and recognition of her status as a woman in the culture of her time appeared in her general poetry as well as her religious reflections.

The first entry in her Sabbath journal occurred in 1819, the last in 1827. During those years she lived first in Port Royal, in the home described above, and later in Fredericksburg, with her mother and sister. Throughout that time period, at least, her life was devoted, almost exclusively, to evangelical Christianity and all it entailed. Though she identified herself as a "lonely Episcopalian" in Port Royal, she joined with every evangelical community gathering in the small town. After an episode with illness she described her return to her "accustomed haunts":

> —the Sanctuary—the Sabbath School—well, she is again restored! the unworthy J.L. is again restored to her usual health and the enjoyment of her usual privileges—again she fills her seat in the Church—again she performs he usual duties at the Sabbath school and again she is able to take her usual walks—the people of God again greet her ...[22]

Rarely did a Sabbath pass when she did not have "the exquisite delight of attending the sanctuary of God." Many times during the week "spiritual society" marked her days.

---

[21]Lomax, "Dreams and Rhapsodies," *Lyre*, 62.

[22]July 30, 1819.

Leadership in the area of Christian education formed another component of her life in the evangelical community. She taught in the Sabbath Schools in Port Royal and, subsequently, in Fredericksburg. Particularly interested in the girls who attended, she implored God "that the dear little lambs entrusted" to her would reap the fruits of heaven. In her home she was "gratified ... in having a family of colour'd Females, to attend in my room during my hours of Prayer, their own voluntary request to do so." Her labors for evangelical Christianity, as "an instrument in the Redeemer's cause," impacted people throughout her little village.[23]

Little deterred Judith Lomax from worshiping, even physical danger. On May 23, [1824] during "a good Sermon from Doc. Sommerville one of the Baptist Brethren," worship took on a new sense of urgency:

> The giving way of the galleries in the Church, caused an alarm, and confusion, in the midst of the discourse, we were obliged to quit the Church, so great was the danger, but we heard the doctor finish his excellent Sermon in the Room of a private house.—Our ill fated Church has now become so dangerous as to prevent the services of Religion being perform'd there—

Even amidst this "great ... confusion" she confidently confessed that her heart "stay'd on the Lord."

In addition to these local evangelical connections, Judith Lomax reached into the larger evangelical world. She subscribed to publications, including *The Washington Theological Repertory*, attended local conventions of Methodist, Episcopal and Baptist denominations, corresponded and visited with missionaries and sent financial contributions to the seminary.[24] As an

---

[23] 9 January n.d.; Sabbath morn., n.d.; Sabbath night, n.d.

[24] "Andrus" was the missionary to whom she referred most frequently, and her relationship with him was, apparently, quite intimate. Many pages in her journal were devoted to their parting and his subsequent death, along with a longing to be reunited with him in heaven. She made an "annual payment of Five dollars to the Theological Seminary in Alexandria for the Education of pious Young Men to the Ministry of the Episcopal Church," 29 March [1826]. Women provided significant financial support to this and other evangelical institutions during the early nineteenth century. For example, in Petersburg, Virginia in 1822, "women of the Presbyterian church established the Education Society to raise money for the training of impoverished young candidates for the ministry. Year in and year out, it was Petersburg's most impressive benevolent association." See Suzanne Lebsock, *The Free Women of Petersburg: Status and Culture in a Southern Town, 1784-1860* (New York: W. W. Norton & Company, 1984), 217.

Episcopalian, Judith Lomax lived during a period of evangelical vitality in her beloved church in Virginia. Two influential, evangelical leaders reestablished the Episcopal Church during the antebellum period in Virginia—Richard Channing Moore and William Meade. At separate points in her journal she indicates attending services over which the two bishops presided and preached. Though the Episcopal Church had languished since the Revolution, these two clergymen influenced the re-building of churches, helped to found the Virginia Theological Seminary in Alexandria, and added significantly to the number of clergy in the state. More importantly to the evangelical Lomax, though, they stressed the doctrines of conversion and revivalism while remaining loyal to the Episcopal tradition. For a "lonely Episcopalian" with an evangelical belief system, these bishops made Virginia a place of ardent religiosity for Judith Lomax.

Her ties to varying facets of the church's world, including publishing, education and missionary endeavors, provided a solid foundation for Lomax's theological growth. She never hesitated to discourse with God on the most mysterious and complex theological issues. As a matter of fact, among the most intriguing passages in her Sabbath journal are theologically complex discussions of Christology, soteriology, eschatology, ecclesiology, the nature of the trinity, epistemology and the proofs of God in creation. One sample should suffice to illustrate the depth of insight revealed in Lomax's Sabbath journal:

> ... we only know that it is in God "we live, and move, and have our being"—
> he hath given to each one of us a soul, and a Body, these *two* act in union in
> each individual, we believe this, we are obliged to do, and that without
> *comprehending* it.—may we not very easily believe the Union of *Three in
> One*, the *Godhead*? We can no more comprehend the *one* than the *other*—
> amethinks then that we might easily believe *three Persons* being *One God* in
> the holy Trinity, when we know of a certainty, how very limited are the
> bounds of Finite comprehension—how unlimited, how unbounded the power
> of Infinite, and Uncreated Excellence ...[25]

This excursus on the Trinity, human knowledge and creation continued for several pages in her journal. Other similar, and even more profound, tracts joined it.

In a cultural ethos concerned that the "wrong mode of education may give the female character a degree of inflation, which passes with superficial people

---

[25]May 12, [1824].

for solidity" and determined that providence "has fitted her to her station ... that subordinate condition, so replete with usefulness and consistency, so suited to the weakness of the sex," Judith Lomax allowed her mind to soar to heights removed from those assigned to her by the world.[26] By 1826 "an extreme langour, and weariness from bad health" plagued Judith Lomax. Though she longed to stay in her "neat and rural habitation," it was time to move. Letters arrived from her sister in Fredericksburg "advising" and "beseeching" her to go and board with her. In early December she determined to sacrifice the home in Port Royal, "where I have sometimes experienced good, and sometimes evil, where I have sometimes experienced painful emotions, and where I have sometimes reposed and dreampt of happiness." The remainder of her life was spent in Fredericksburg, and she worshiped regularly at St. George Episcopal Church, under the leadership of the familiar "Rev. Mr. McGuire ... whom I now consider as my pastor."[27]

Judith Lomax spent the last year of her life as she had spent many before, praising God, teaching Sunday School, attending the Episcopal Convention which was held in Fredericksburg in 1827, reading and writing about her theological queries, and preparing to die. In 1828, "all in readiness for the heavenly Bridegroom" and prepared to "win on a buoyant step my airy way, seeking the bosom of my Father," Judith Lomax died. Her obituary attested to the community's recognition of her religious quest:

> DIED Suddenly in this town, on Friday last, Miss Judith Lomax: ill health had in a great measure prepared the deceased and surviving friends for her removal from this world. The period of decline had not, however, been suffered to pass unimproved. There was on her part a sincere and diligent attention to all those things which concern the peace of the soul and there was an earnestness in some good degree corresponding with the magnitude of the interest at stake. Devout and benevolent she evinced in her life the practical energy of the religion embraced by her; nor was her benevolence of the doubtful or ordinary kind; it was discriminating, uniform and self-denying; and she has descended to the grave very favourably and gratefully remembered by societies and individuals, who for years have shared her

---

[26]Virginia Cary, *Letters on Female Character* (Richmond: A. Works, 1828), Rare Publications Collection, Virginia Historical Society, Richmond, Virginia, 21.

[27]November 1, 1826; November 22, 1826; December 4, 1826.

habitual and systematic benefactions. "Pleased are the dead who die for the Lord, for they rest from their labour and their works do follow them."[28]

In addition to this testimony, a brief listing of the Lomax family provides clues to her unique devotion. It states that Judith Lomax died "at Fredericksburg, 1828 January 19, and was buried in the churchyard at St. George's."[29] Of the fourteen family members on the list, only this entry recorded a burial place, attesting to the significance of the fact that she lay to rest in her beloved churchyard.

The Sabbath Journal of Judith Lomax

Held in the manuscript collection of the Virginia Historical Society in Richmond, Virginia, the journal of Judith Lomax serves as a rare first-hand glimpse into the life of a woman in early nineteenth-century America. The original proves somewhat problematic in its current condition. While series of pages are perfectly preserved and remain in chronological order, others are fragmented and gathered together in an arbitrary manner. As with most journals of the time period, the spelling and punctuation do not conform to late twentieth-century standards; the original form is retained in this transcription. The reader must also remember that these are personal pieces, not intended, necessarily, for a broad readership. Therefore, in their original form such journals as this remain, obviously, unedited and unpolished.

Judith Lomax's journal constitutes a source of unique interest for a variety of reasons: the time period covered, her economic situation, her social place within society and her intensely complex and developed theological mind.

First, she lived during the years of the early Republic, in the cultural center of the South, and one could argue of the entire early American Republic—the state of Virginia. Evangelicalism was just beginning to assume a position of acceptability and prominence during the first quarter of the nineteenth century, having been primarily a movement peripheral to the

---

[28]*Virginia Herald*, January 23, 1828.

[29] Listing held at the Virginia Historical Society. Unfortunately, though I have examined, along with assistants, all of the headstones in the cemetery of St. George's Episcopal Church in Fredericksburg, the one for Judith Lomax cannot be located. Many headstones from the time period during which she was buried have been worn to the point that the inscriptions are not legible. One can assume from all other evidence, however, that one of these headstones is that of Lomax.

dominant religion of the influential.[30] Virginia still held the tradition of the Protestant Episcopal Church as paramount, but was wrestling with the ever-expanding influence of evangelicalism. Most of the initial adherents to evangelicalism hailed from the lower classes of society or were women or African slaves. Often seen as threatening to the ruling authorities, they were subjected to ridicule and harsh treatment. In turn, evangelicals condemned those of wealth, status and power as being attached to the pleasures of the world rather than devoted to true Christianity. Indeed, evangelicalism continued its strong appeal to these characteristically dominated components of society throughout its early history.

Scholarly consensus as to the exact nature of the interplay of religious forces during these very years has yet to be achieved. Nathan Hatch, for instance, argues that between the years 1780 and 1830 an indelible imprint was left upon the structure of both American Christianity and political life as the message of evangelical conversion joined with that of the democratic vocabularies of politics to "democratize" Christianity. On the other hand, Jon Butler argues that formal institutions, such as the established Protestant Episcopal Church, marked the most influential religious aspect of the time.[31] As Judith Lomax wrote, she also struggled with the theological issues inherent in the move from a hierarchical, institutional establishment to the more egalitarian evangelical establishment.

Yet within a few generations, most historians concur that evangelicalism itself became the respectable form of Christianity for southerners, slave or free, male or female, rich or poor. Not only did those aspects of the culture which had earlier rejected evangelicalism and its methods, such as the Protestant Episcopal

---

[30]The most recent work which proposes the initial resistance to evangelicalism in the South in the late eighteenth and early nineteenth centuries is Christine Leigh Heyrman, *Southern Cross: The Beginnings of the Bible Belt* (Knopf: 1997).

[31]In addition the recent work by Heyrman, see: John Boles, "Evangelical Protestantism in the Old South: From Religious Dissent to Cultural Dominance," in *Evangelical Protestantism in the South*, ed. Charles Wilson (Jackson: University Press of Mississippi, 1985); Robert Calhoun, *Evangelicals and Conservatives in the Early South, 1740-1861* (Columbia: University of South Carolina Press, 1988); Rhys Isaac, *The Transformation of Virginia* (Chapel Hill: University of North Carolina Press, 1982); Anne Loveland, *Southern Evangelicals and the Social Order: 1800-1860* (Baton Rouge: Louisiana State University Press); Nathan Hatch, *The Democratization of American Christianity* (New Haven: Yale University Press, 1989); Jon Butler, *Awash in a Sea of Faith* (Cambridge: Harvard University Press, 1990).

establishment, adapt to evangelicalism, but evangelicalism adapted to the genteel world to a certain degree. Evidence of refinement and organization emerged in evangelical worship settings. Previously characterized by "jerks" and "extravagancies," worship ritual increasingly displayed an extent of formality and apparent normalcy. Though revivals, protracted meetings and camp meetings still occurred regularly, they were instituted as "sober and regular forms of worship."[32] Anxious benches remained within the worship setting and focus on conversion never ceased, but the emotionality of the events seemed to wane.

Judith Lomax wrote as a self-designated "lonely Episcopalian," who lived in the flux of the period. Though a dedicated member of her own denominational communion, she enthusiastically attended any worship service available in her small town of Port Royal, Virginia and accepted the power of the Word, regardless of the denomination of the preacher. Often the preacher was a Baptist, Methodist or Presbyterian, and, when appropriate, she hailed their truly "evangelical" character, placing her clearly within this religious movement:

> Heard yesterday two very good and very Evangelical sermons from the Rev. Mr. Morrison, the young Presbyterian, his subjects are well adapted and well calculated to do good in Port Royal, if those who are the hearers, would also, be the doers of the word, but alas how very few ever of those who profess to be followers of the glorious Redeemer live up to their privileges—I feel my shortcomings.[33]

Still, she longed for the rituals of her own Protestant Episcopal communion. This places her squarely within the flux of the tradition and of the culture of the time. As an evangelical, she was one of those on the periphery moving towards the center of culture and adapting to rather outstanding ecumenical lifestyles. As an ardent Episcopalian, she remained within the dominant and traditional culture of the Early Republic in Virginia. She sometimes precariously straddled and other times comfortably bridged the two religious worldviews—one filled with traditional liturgy and elite culture, the other with the enthusiasm of conversion and revival. Occasionally, the culture's religious transformation caused pain for

---

[32]"The Injury Done to Religion by Ignorant Preachers: A Sermon Delivered Before an Education Society in September 1825," *Virginia Evangelical and Literary Magazine*, November 1825, 603. See also Donald Mathews, *Religion in the Old South* (Chicago: University of Chicago Press, 1977), chapter 3, "An Enlightened and Refined People."

[33]Lomax, Monday morning, n.d., 1819.

Lomax as is obvious in the description given of a prayer meeting she attended in Port Royal:

> ...there are in this place, some of what are call'd the lower order, who profess themselves Christians, I frequently associate with them, because they converse with me on my favorite subject, the Love of God!—Those who compose this little society, are Baptists and Methodist, they are illiterate, and I being of another denomination, do not feel completely at home with them.—I seem to stand every way alone, in this wide world; in this little Village I am alone;—it is true there are some here, who call themselves Episcopalians, but I differ from *them*, as much as I do from the Baptists and Methodists...[34]

Her intense devotion led to a religious world of confusion and frustration as she attempted to reconcile her own spirituality with that of the institutions surrounding her.

In terms of her economic situation, Lomax also provides a poignant and relevant picture. Many of the extant journals from the antebellum period were composed by women of privileged economic status, thus raising questions about their significance for determining the religious experience of the majority of women within the culture.[35] Lomax, however, was not particularly affluent. Having been estranged from her prestigious family she lived in a modest home, which she referred to as her "own little dwelling." This "neat and rural habitation," into which she apparently sought to take boarders to cover her expenses, seemed to be the only place of refuge which she had. When her health was failing, in the fall of 1826, she stated:

> I seem to think it is not the will of the Lord for me to quit my residence in Port Royal, for I know of no place at this time where I could get boarded and believing it his will I am content to remain here, and have even made some exertion to get the necessary comforts for the approach of Winter.—to do thy will, O my God, is all my pleasure!—[36]

---

[34]Lomax, Monday Morning, [January 30, 1820].

[35]See, for example, the other journal which I have noted, that of Caroline Homassel Thornton who was the mistress of a large plantation overlooking the Rappahannock River in Virginia.

[36]Lomax, November 10 [1826].

From this statement, and other general information regarding her life, it is evident that Lomax was required to deal with the needs of everyday survival. These mundane activities and financial concerns are the province of the "ordinary" person rather than of the upper echelons of society.

Finally, the theological complexity and historical value of her journal places it in the company of such women as Margery Kempe, Jane Hoskens, Jarena Lee, Elizabeth Ashbridge, Elizabeth White and Old Elizabeth.[37] Lomax addresses issues of eschatology, ecclesiology, conversion, soteriology, Christology, Trinitarian theology, creation theology, divine providence and intercession and missiology. One passage, dealing with epistemology, provides a clear example of the complex theological content of her journal and witnesses to the fact that laity—lay women even—did engage in intense theological discourse worthy of study by others:

> ... that I know not how we are bound to comprehend all that we believe—does not every day's experience of the powers of the great God of the Universe prove to us that we with our feeble powers of capacity *cannot*—can we understand the wonderful works of Creation daily operating before our eyes?—let us begin with the vegetative tribe, from the tender blade of grass just shooting its green head above the soil, and growing, and maturing, until it scatters its fruitful seed around,—for the majestic Oak, first shewing itself a little leafy tendril, then growing and maturing, until its lofty boughs overshadow our heads, and its fruitful honors are scatter'd on the ground, that other Oaks, the pride of the Forest may be again produced, a shade for Man and Beast—{....} all produced by the great Author of Nature, but we know not how—we believe, are obliged by optical demonstration [...] these things *are*, but we know not how they are, we do not *comprehend* them.—From the vegetative, we might go to the Brute creation—not only to the Brute Creation, but to the Feather'd creation, the Fowl's of the air, and descend from them, to the Reptile, and Insect tribes.—these are all of them produced by a Master's

---

[37]*The Book of Margery Kempe* (1436-1438), this work was recently studied by Ellen Ross, "Spiritual Experience and Women's Autobiography: The Rhetoric of Selfhood in the Book of Margery Kempe," *Journal of the American Academy of Religion* 59:3, 527-546; Jane Hoskens, *The Life and Spiritual Sufferings of That Faithful Servant of Christ* (Philadelphia: 1771); *The Life and religious Experience of Jarena Lee, a Coloured Lady, Giving an Account of Her Call to Preach the Gospel. Revised and Correctd from the Original Manuscript, Written by Herself* (early 1800s), reprinted in Andrews, *Sisters of the Spirit; Some Account of the Life of Elizabeth Ashbridge ... Wrote by Herself* (Philadelphia: 1774); *The Experiences of God's Gracious Dealings with Mrs. Elizabeth White* (1741); *Memoir of Old Elizabeth: A Coloured Woman* (Philadelphia: Collins, Printer, 1863), reprinted in *Six Women's Slave Narratives* (Oxford: Oxford University Press, 1988).

hand—we know that they *are*, but we do not know *how* they are,—we do not *comprehend* them.—we are obliged to believe that which is so wonderful as to be far beyond the feeble powers of our comprehension.—we believe that we ourselves [...] we are obliged to believe it, we *know* that it cannot admit of a doubt, and we know still more we know that we have a vital principle within us which acts upon the body.—that is we know for we *feel* that we have a Body, and a Soul, acting one upon the other.—we do know that we are "fearfuly, and wonderfuly made." but we do not know *how*, we cannot *comprehend* it.—we only know that it is in God "we live, and move, and have our being."—he hath given to each one of us a soul, and a Body, these *two* act in union in each individual, we believe this, which we are obliged to do, and that without *comprehending* it.—may we not very easily believe the Union of *Three in One*, in the *Godhead*? we can no more comprehend the *one* than the *other*—methinks then that we might easily believe *three Persons* being *One God* in the holy Trinity, w hen we know of a certainty, how very limited are the bounds of Finite comprehension—how unlimited, how unbounded the power of Infinite, and Uncreated Excellence-[38]

Lomax expounds on theological issues with a depth of wisdom rarely recognized in women or men of her day. Her journal provides evidence for such complex theological reflection among some antebellum southern women.

Judith Lomax and the Experience of Love Mysticism

Love mysticism is a unique sub-category of mystical experience which emerges throughout human history and in a variety of world religions. For example, marriage mysticism in Hindu bhakti literature describes the female devotee as "none other than the woman in love who lamented any separation from her beloved, her chosen deity, and ecstatically rejoiced in union with him."[39] Rabi'a, an early Islamic love mystic, explored the "hitherto forbidden territory of reciprocal, though perhaps not precisely mutual, divine-human love" in her incredible poetry dedicated to her love for Allah.[40] The language of these

---

[38]Lomax, May 12, [1825]. An extended portion was removed from the text included. The reader is directed to the above portion of Lomax's journal, which includes a four-page theological exposition related to Trinitarian theology, original sin, creation theology, faith and epistemology.

[39]Katherine Young, "Hinduism," in *Women in World Religions*, ed. Arvind Sharma (Albany: State University of New York Press, 1987), 77.

[40]John Renard, *Seven Doors to Islam* (Berkeley: University of California Press, 1996), 110.

particular mystics expresses an erotic, all-consuming yearning for their divine Beloved that engulfs them and defines who they are and what they do.

One of the most prominent, graphically written, and later visually portrayed, experiences of love mysticism within the Christian tradition is that of Teresa of Avila. She describes her encounter with her divine lover as both agonizing and ecstatic:

> In his hands I saw a long golden spear and at the end of the iron tip I seemed to see a point of fire. With this he appeared to pierce my heart several times so that it penetrated to my entrails. When he drew the spear out, I thought he was drawing the entrails out with it, leaving me completely afire with a great love for God. The pain was so sharp that it made me utter several moans; and so excessive was the sweetness of this intense pain that I wished never to lose it.[41]

Teresa's love mysticism led her to a state of physical pleasure and pain, which could be interpreted as reaching the heights of orgasm.

Love mysticism involves a new understanding of the self, a new subjectivity. As the mystic becomes the beloved of the divine and God becomes the beloved of her or of him, she is redefined, elevated and enhanced beyond any concepts that her previous humanity provided. As the "Spouse of God," the love mystic reaches levels of consciousness and understanding through being the divine consort.

Unlike the heights of ecstasy disclosed in love mysticism, antebellum evangelical Christianity in the American South defined women as totally subservient to and ultimately connected with the male-dominated society. Women were to have a "thorough and practical acquaintance with the arts and duties of domestic life ... they adorn and beautify the most distinguished of her sex..."[42] Yearning for their divine lover and accepting their Heavenly Spouse's presence in their chambers were not aspects of this prescribed evangelical

---

[41]Teresa of Avila, "Life," in *The Collected Works of Saint Teresa of Avila*, vol. 1, trans. Kavanaugh and Rodriguez (Washington, D.C.: 1976), 193-194. This experience was expressed visually by Bernini in his erotic rendering of the scene.

[42]"Valuable Suggestion," *The Washington Theological Repertory* (December 1827): 758-759. The introduction to this piece reads in an equally intriguing manner: "But we forbear;—the voice of Fashion is louder and possessed of a stronger charm than ours; and, as long as Custom bids, we expect to see fathers educating their daughters to be for other men such wives as they could never wish for themselves."

behavior in the pre-Civil War South. Though evangelicals focused on an individual relationship with the divine, it took the form of pragmatic devotion and the communally oriented conversion experience.

It was strongly suggested by men and women alike that they fill their roles without question or doubt. One evangelical woman emphatically reiterated this position:

> I can safely declare to woman, with the Bible in my hand, that her husband is to have rule over her. If she is found in her appointed sphere of duty, she may expect a blessing; but if she strikes out a new and strange way for herself, she is left to the uncovenanted mercies of her Maker.[43]

Striking out a new and strange way left her beyond the realm of human approval and estranged from eternal mercy and salvation.

Marriage was described as the "perfect trial ground for both republican and religious virtue."[44] The institution served political, social and religious ends, as such it was believed to be the proper state. An *Essay on Old Maids* was circulated to further degrade the status of perpetually single women suggesting, in this three volume work, that women should "yield freedom, render obedience, and pay homage" to a husband or experience the "dark side" of life.[45] In a world constructed around an intensely hierarchical society—slave and free, husband and wife, black and white, servant and master—staying within these well-defined roles provided the means for preservation of the structure and for the maintenance of order.

In the midst of this praise of the state of matrimony, the religious ethos stressed the separation of the converted from the evils of worldly society. Human sexuality, especially, became a persistent and terrifying personal problem. Natural responses and desires became for evangelical Christians an ominous threat of hell-fire, as the forces of good and evil fought for possession of their immortal souls. Exemplified by the mulatto, the child of what was

---

[43]Virginia Cary, 23.

[44]For an extended essay on this topic see Anya Jabour, "No Fetters But Such as Love Shall Forge," *Virginia Magazine of History and Biography* 104:2 (Spring 1996): 211-250.

[45]Suggested by Michael O'Brien, *An Evening When Alone: Four Journals of Single Women in the South, 1827-67* (Charlottesville: University Press of Virginia, 1993). See in particular the diary of Elizabeth Ruffin, 1 March 1827, in O'Brien's edition.

considered the disgraceful union of black and white, the danger of the erotic became evident and, thus, passion was tightly repressed. One Methodist bishop, who obviously wrestled with this temptation himself, proclaimed:

> Therefore avoid the allurements of Voluptuousness, and fly every temptation that leads to her banquet as you would the devil himself. Oh how she spreads her board with delicacies. Her wine sparkles, her dainties invite, her Mirth charms. Which opens a door to more dangers... Lascivious love stands in her bower. She spreads her temptations & begins to court their regard. Her limbs are soft and delicate; her attire loose & inviting, wantonness sparkles in her eyes. She woos with her looks and by the smoothness of her tongue endeavors to deceive.

Anxiety and trepidation surrounded the issue of sexuality. In this context the southern evangelical woman was to "behave in an appropriate manner among appropriate people to achieve appropriate goals." This could be achieved through "refined manners and pious attitudes."[46]

Appropriateness did not constitute Judith Lomax's highest priority and she broke this mode in significant ways. Although unwavering in her faith and evangelicalism, her experience of love mysticism and definition of herself as the "Spouse of God" redefined how she understood herself in relation to both God and humanity. Both her present self and that which she imaged for eternity was transformed by her mystical experience:

> ...he knows my desire, and my groanings are not hid from him—oh, I trust he will speed the time when I shall be completely sanctified to him!—when I shall be ripe for glory, and worthy of being admitted into his heavenly kingdom, there to dwell in his presence forever,—to live forever around his Throne ... Oh, how my waking meditations, and even my sleeping visions, delight to dwell on these things ...[47]

In her "secret chambers, from the watchings of her inmost soul," her mystical experience emerged.[48] Unlike the "daughters of vanity" who prepared for "flattering admirers at the nocturnal hour," Lomax awaited the coming of Christ, her "heavenly Bride groom." She desired to "be cloathed by thee, clad in white –

---

[46]Donald Mathews, *Religion in the Old South*, 62, 120.

[47]Lomax, January 29, 1820.

[48]Lomax, September 24, [1823].

array'd in the wedding garment." Her preoccupation with assuming the eternal gender role of "Sainted Maid in heaven" made this vision the central focus of her existence and she inquired ardently of God:

> When shall I be perfected unto holiness!—when shall I be a beatified spirit, dwelling in the presence of God eternally!—a Sainted Maid...—The Spouse of God!

She called for the One "whom my soul lovest—my company, my comforter, my only friend" to come to her. Then, "shall appear that heaven of love" and she could "dwell with [Jesus] without a veil between!" Eternity with her beloved Bride groom consumed her hopes.[49]

Judith Lomax affirmed herself as both "Spouse of God" and "bride of Christ." She was "the Apple of his [Christ's] eye." One intriguing Christmas meditation emphasized her sense of mystical union with the divine as both intimate and unique, as well as filling the requisite criteria of being an immediate experience of the divine:

> Come O, my Saviour come, draw near to me thou Prince of peace, and take up thine abode in my heart—fill up the space in my secret Chambers, and manifest thyself to me, not as thou dost unto the world—behold thy lowly hand maid retired far from the [noise and] revelry of a tumultuous world, she would hold communion with none but thee ... **the world hath not known thee; but I ha[ve] known thee.**[50]

She knew God as the "world" did not and she determined that she would unite with God exclusively.

As her lifelong passion increased, along with her desire to maintain herself as a "Virgin" in order to be "prepared for her heavenly bridegroom," so did her imagery intensify. God came to her in more intimate and immediate ways. She described the experience here in third person:

> ...it is his whispering spirit, that speaketh to her spirit, at Morn, and Noon, and setting Sun, and even in the watchings of the Night, biding her be *Holy*, to keep her Lamp ready trim'd, and burning for that she shall "know neither the

---

[49]Lomax, December 8, 1822; [December 1823]; [January 1822]; January 24, [1823]; January [1822].

[50]Lomax, Christmas 1824.

day, nor the hour wherein the Son of Man cometh."—it bideth her in whispers soft and sweet, to be prepared to meet the heavenly Bridegroom,—there is One,—a lonely beam!—but the Lord careth for it, he looketh down from heaven upon its—with his breath he reneweth the oft times expiring embers,—thus lighting up a fresh, the flame his love had kindled,—he careth for the bruised reed!—Precious Jesus, that should thus take account of that lonely one in her secret Chambers!

Eventually, with her "lamp ready trim'd" and "burning red" in anticipation, she heard the voice of God say to her, "Judith prepare thee," and she responded:

...and shall I not be prepared for the heavenly Bridegroom?—forbid it thou great Immanuel—forbid it the triune God!—oh aid me to keep y lamp ready trim'd! Let me be the wise Virgin, all in readiness for the heavenly Bridegroom.[51]

Judith Lomax's dramatic and developed mystical experience is echoed in other journals, but hers is expressed most explicitly and intensely.

The expression of this powerful experience of love mysticism in a culture which had not overtly cultivated such a sensual encounter with the divine seems revolutionary. Regarding the construction of love mysticism in this setting it is apparent that women, who understood their identity, even and especially their public religious identity, in relationship to men, extended this into the realm of the divine. They entered into eternal marriage with God. In that sense, they were still fulfilling the wifely role prescribed to them by society. As such, the imagery may not seem terribly spectacular.

But, simultaneously suppressed and restricted by society, such women became sensual beings worthy of the erotic and mutual love of God. As "Spouse of God" and "bride of Christ," chosen by the divine and knowing God as the "world hath not," their marginality on earth was absolved into a mystical relationship. As Hadewijch embraced and was embraced by her divine lover, as Beatrice prepared to be the Spouse of Heaven, as Teresa gave herself, body and soul, to the ecstasy of the divine, so did Judith Lomax. By claiming the significance of herself as the feminine consort of the divine, Lomax rose above the role to which she was consigned, even to claim the intense satisfaction of God's presence about her bed. While she reimagined herself as "bride of Christ" she gained a sense of self far transcending anything her culture could offer. This first-hand testimony to the experience of love mysticism in such a powerful

---

[51]Lomax, January 1, [1824]; January 26, [1823].

fashion provides scholars new insight into the evangelical world of the antebellum South.

Because of its place in the definition of a new genre, its contribution to the study of religion in the American South, its intriguing possibilities in terms of the phenomenon of love mysticism, and, most importantly, its ability to open the window into the life of a unique, but ordinary, woman, this journal promises to become central to many studies of women and religion in the Old South. Hopefully its readers can grasp the passion of its composer at least partially.

Editorial Principles

In editing this journal, I have chosen to follow the pattern established by Michael O'Brien in the volume he edited for the Southern Texts Society, *An Evening When Alone: Four Journals of Single Women in the South, 1827-67*. His editorial principles transfer well to Lomax's journal. First, I will attempt to omit nothing from the original manuscript and remain dedicated to the original spelling, punctuation, capitalization and underlining. This may lead to some confusion because of nontraditional spellings. When a divergent spelling causes such confusion [sic] will be employed. But this will be done sparingly, only when necessary to clarify a statement, so as not to break the flow of the original texts. When the composer of the journal uses her own emphases within the text, such as underlining or capitalizing, those will be retained. If I choose to emphasize something that she has not, such will be indicated in notation.

Certain exceptions, as chosen by O'Brien, will be employed. The form of dating is standardized for each journal entry. Thus, "Jan.ry 29" (no year, as Judith Lomax rarely included the year with her journal entry) will read "January 29, 1825." On occasion the date was reconstructed based upon internal evidence and context. Those dates that could not be reconstructed definitively are enclosed in brackets, i.e. [January 29, 1825] or January 29, [1825]. And, as explained by O'Brien, "on the occasions when the original text is too confused to make this possible, I have defined the range of options." Some undated passages are inserted, for example segments entitled "Fragments." In these cases, the note reflects the title given in the journal itself. Other times it has been impossible to reconstruct a date and no apparent title is given. On these occasions, as the reader may have already seen in notations, "n.d." indicates "no date." Although I have paginated the journal for ease of reference, these are not indicative of page numbers in the original manuscript, which bears no such formality.

Sometimes, because of the possible loss of important material, there are illegible words and missing or torn passages. Again I follow O'Brien: [...] means a single word is illegible and [....] means more than a single word; {...} means a short torn passage and {....} means a long one. On occasion I have been able to identify a missing word or a portion of a missing word from the context, but in these cases the reconstructed word will always be denoted by brackets, for example [and] or [of]ten.

In addition, the lengths of dashes, though they "vary wildly" in the original manuscripts, have been standardized. Dashes are of "the essence of nineteenth century punctuation," therefore periods have not been inserted though it would be convenient and tempting to do so.[52]

One change in this strictly authentic reconstruction of the format has been made, however. Often, Judith Lomax would underline words for emphasis, those words have been italicized for publication as such is more conducive for the purposes of both printer and reader.

Primarily the goal is to maintain the integrity of the journal as written by this fascinating nineteenth century evangelical woman. Underlined words or phrases and italicized or bold print will be reflected as in the journal itself, unless otherwise delineated. Whenever rare exceptions exist to these rules, and to the primary goal of reflecting the journals themselves, they will be noted.

---

[52]Michael O'Brien, ed. *An Evening When Alone*, 49-51.

The Note Book,
Or Diary, of Judith Lomax

• 1819 •

And may that name, although of little note on Earth, may it—oh, may it
be recorded in a Fairer Book than this!—even in the Book of Life!

Heavenly Father! look on me the humblest of thy creatures,—inscribe on
my heart, holiness unto thee—and keep me—oh keep me—Ever thine![53]

And oh may that [name mere][54] and insignificant, as it is here on Earth,—
oh may it be enrol'd [in a] fairer Book than this!—even now, may I hope that it
stands recorded in [the] Book of Life!—Heavenly Father! look on me the
humblest of thy Creatures [and] keep me, Ever Thine!—"O learn me true
understanding and knowledge, [I] have believed thy commandments."—"I have
apply'd my heart to fulfil thy statutes alway, even unto the end."—"O let my
heart be sound in thy [sight] that I be not ashamed."—"Thou art about my path,
and about my bed, and [spiest] out all my ways!"—"Try me, oh God, and seek
the ground of my heart, [probe] and examine my thoughts!"—"Thy testimonies,
oh Lord, are very sure, [holy] becometh thine house forever."—"The Lord is my
shepherd; therefore can I lack nothing."—"I will say unto the Lord, thou art my
hope, and my strong hold, my [God] in him will I trust."—"Stablish me with thy
free spirit."—"Take not thy holy spirit from me."—Heavenly Father! inscribe on
my heart Holiness unto the Lord."—yea Lord, complete thy work, and sanctify
me wholly!—J.L.[55]

---

[53] All spelling, punctuation and other emphases in the text remain from the original,
with the previously noted exception of underlining which has been replaced by italicized type
throughout. In addition, dates have been standardized to a certain extent (e.g. "Jan.ry"
becomes "January"). Although there are numerous spellings that do not conform to late
twentieth-century norms, as mentioned in the introduction, [sic] will be avoided in order to
allow the text to flow.

[54] Words in brackets have been inserted based on the surrounding text and those
portions which can be deciphered, however the brackets do indicate such reconstruction of
the text by the editor and are, therefore, educated conjecture.

[55] J.L.—Judith Lomax; occasionally throughout the diary she signs her name at the
end of an entry, most often when it is an entry marked "fragments" and thus not assigned a
particular date.

An Invocation

Oh, holy ghost! spirit divine!
Come breathe thy sacred influence here,
Guide thou this trembling heart of mine,
In grief, or joy still hover near.
When with the first bright beam of morn,
Night's airy visions fade away;
To thou illume my day new-born
And shed abroad a brighter way.
So shall a pure, and ardent flame,
Kindle the prayer, the song of praise;
The Prayer which in a Saviour's name,
Is incense at a Throne of Grace.
And still while ling'ring in the West,
Appears the last faint beam Ev'n:
then holy Spirit fill my breast,
and waft the contrite prayer to Heav'n.
Won by a Saviour's dying love,
Oh! may I catch one ray divine;
And fixing all my thoughts above,
Be holy Spirit !—Ever Thine!

[March] 18, 1819—A Meditation,—A Covenant[56]

"I am thine, save me, for I have sought thy price[...]—Yes, dearest Lord, to thee I dedicate myself, for whom have I [outside] thee?—and who else is capable of filling my vast desires?—{....}[57] by repeated surrenders of myself, by {....}

{....} I am by every {....}tion, by Grace, by Love.—[...] may I not [...] are these the delusions of feeling? or am I indeed accepted?[...] Lord and Saviour! pour into my mind a right knowledge,[...] to understand, and oh! let me

---

[56] When year is included with the date it is a replication of such in the original text, in other words the date has been written in Lomax's hand. She rarely included the year with the entire date, therefore when such is included it became a primary tool for reconstructing chronological order.

[57] This extended bracket—{....}—indicates a portion of the text that may be several words in length and which is damaged beyond reconstruction, or is missing entirely because of torn pages.

have the witnesing of thy ho[nor] that I may know I am indeed thine, wholly
unalterably thine [no] idol usurp thy place, banish every earthly feeling, and [...]
oh! make my heart a temple worthy of recieving a Saviour [...] worthy of his
Love, worthy of his divine mediation, let it [be ti]ed forever by the breathings of
his holy spirit then come Lo[rd re]cieve the offering,—"Make haste my beloved
and be thou lik[e ...], or to a young hart on the mountains of spices," if thou
[were] mine, I have nothing else to ask,

> "Give what thou wilt, without thee I am poor
> Take what thou wilt, and with thee I am rich"

Why do thy Chariot wheels delay?—oh come and array me in thy robes of
righteousness, let my soul be adorn'd with the ornaments of brightness and
hasten thy coming my beloved!—Pleasant to me [are thy] ordinances, and all
that brings me nearer to thee.—I love [thee] [...] and the place where thine honor
dwelleth.—Grateful to my [...] thy word, I love to receive it, and to receive it
from the lips [of thy] faithful servants, thy own embassadors! then is it sweet to
me [much] sweeter than honey, or the spangled dew drop of the morn, when [in]
all its purity it falls in balmy freshness from the first Rose of early [spring] on
the bosom of the earth.—And oh! for the blessed presence of [my] Lord and
Saviour on the ensuing Sabbath!—may he be amongst [...] we through *faith*
receive him! and may the sacred repast pre[pare] [...] be to the refreshing of
many souls!—oh that my soul may [...] at my Father's Table! may he give me to
eat of the bread [...] of Life! and while with sacred awe I approach his board [...]
in grateful humility think of all he has done for me, and [look] [...] more and
more.—Oh may the solemn Covenant that shall there [be m]ade, bind me more
strongly to him!—may he set his [...] seal upon it!—may it bind me his forever!
Judith Lomax

{....}angels have witness'd {....} the solemn dedication.—how I but that
the spirit of my once earthly, but I hope now [saintly self] Father, in its beatified
state might at that moment have hover'd and smiled upon me?—oh, it was a
blessed moment! And [...][58] with a few of the faithful I approach'd the sacred
Table [...] methought the Saviour himself beckon'd us on, and with [...]
welcomed our approach—Often have I recieved the sac[ra-] ments before, but it
appear'd to me that I then recieved [them] for the first time;—whence was
this?—was it that grace [had] indeed renew'd my heart? or was it that the sacred
ordinance more solemnly, more feelingly administer'd than I had ever be[fore]

---

[58] This bracket within the text indicates that perhaps one or two words are missing,
oftentimes when the edge of a page has been torn off.

known it?—Cold indeed must that heart have been, who could have remain'd unmoved during the eloquent and affe[cting] discourse deliver'd by our pious, and excellent young Pastor, surely the Lord was with him!—and rested his blessing upon [him]—And now my "Father who art in heaven" enable me to [...] Covenant which I have so lately made; without thee I can [...] thing,—more than ever do I feel my own insufficiency, [and] need of a Saviour, but I have placed my trust on a sure fo[undation] for tho I am helpless, yet *thou* art *all sufficient.* and hast [thou] not said, "mine own will I keep"?—then keep me Lord in [thy] ways, and let the remaining years of my Life be devoted [to] thy service, and thy cause only teach me what I shall [do to] serve thee, let me be but an instrument in thy hands to [do thy] will.—a weak instrument I must surely be! but [tho] weak, yet *thou* art strong,—yes, thou art omnipotent [...]—and "save *me* for I have sought thy precepts."—I [have] dared to covenant with thee!—my Lord I thank thee! [...] done all things well!—my prayer has been answer'd, I h[ave eaten] the sacred bread,—again have I tasted of thy [...]—Pleasant, yea very pleasant to my remembr[ance ...] of March.—Blessed be the name of the Lord [...]

Judith Lomax

March 22, 1819

And has it then pass'd? have I indeed covenanted with my Lord?—yes *I feel* that the sacred compact has been [made], that he has set his own witnessing seal upon it,—before an [...] led company of my fellow mortals I have acknowledged my [beloved], have declared myself one amongst the number of his faithful [followers].—but *more* than *the world,*—an {....} recorded {....} {....} and at the last, may he bring me to his heavenly rest, where there is fullness of joy, and life forevermore.—oh may I at the last, come to his eternal joy, and dwell forevermore where Jesus is!

Fragments[59]

To admire, to esteem, to love, are congenial to my nature [...] unhappy because the affections are not brought into exercise [...] narrate abstract

---

[59]The title for this section—"Fragments"—is written in Lomax's hand and seems to be inserted at this point in the original text. Other pages/portions with the same designation are placed at the end of the journal in this edition, though in the extant journal they are interspersed throughout and do not seem to be placed in their original locations.

perfection requires a vigorous exertion of the [...] powers—I would have virtue exemplified, I would love it in my [...] Creatures, I would catch the glorious enthusiasm, and rise [...] created, to uncreated excellence.—I love the great Creator, [...] and admire him through his works.—I would fain love and [...] him thro *all* his Works.—oh for a view of *created* excellence[...]

I daily perceive the gay and the [...] among my sex amused with every passing trifle, gratified [...] routine of heartless, mindless intercourse; fully occupied, [...] by domestic employment, or the childish vanity of varying [...] ornaments, and hanging drapery on a smooth black.—I [...] to dispise, and I regularly practise the necessary avocations [...] neither am I superior to the vanitys; the habits acquire [...] precepts, and example adhere tenaciously, and are never [...] by eradicated, But all these are insufficient to engross, [...] the aspiring active mind.—that mind still looks beyond [...] seek this world.

Monday Night, May 21
"Time's rapid moments soon compel,
The saints to bid the last farewell,"
This day I have experienced the "rending smart" of parting forever [in] this world with a spiritual friend, and brother in Christ, a meek and lowly servant of the blessed Jesus,—yes, the Pastor in whom I have delighted, he whose spiritual converse has so often been the means of elevating my thoughts to heaven, has now forever left this corner of the vineyard [...] I hope we shall meet again in those blissful abodes, where all cause for parting is done away, where the weary are at rest," and where in the presence of God there is "fulness of joy forevermore."

In this world where *all* is so imperfect, where even our best delights, our purest affections, are mingled with alloy, how often do we find, oh! we *always* find, that the love of the *creature* is but the *shade* of happiness, while the love of the *Creator is happiness supreme*—how often has my fond heart whispered to my erring judgement, that my pursuits were pure, were laudable, that they originated in the love of God! but perhaps this has been self love which as given to my own mind.

August 4
Have heard with very great satisfaction an excellent discourse from the celebrated Mr. Broadus, of the Baptist Church. Well, since I cannot hear the ministers of my own particular branch of the Christian Church, I [...] thankfully glean what I can from others—and may the Lord enable me to find profit in so

doing, Have twice attended the Sabbath School since my late indisposition—
may my heavenly Father, by his spirit, keep me ever in the path of duty—surely
I am only spared that I may perform his will! Perhaps he has seen fit to prolong
my days that I may work for God in his cause! Then may I be more, and more
devoted [to] him—may he "direct me in my going out, and my coming in."

August 28

Have been listening to the Preached Word from the Methodist brethren,
who have held their quarterly meeting in this Village,—oh, may it have been to
the profit of my soul, and to that of many others!—Not having the privileges of
my own Church. I feel grateful for any profit I may derive from others.—and
have been gratified at having the pleasure of entertaining some of the Ministers,
besides others of the people of God in my house during the time of their stay in
the Village.—it is very delightful to me the communion of Christians, even
though they may not belong to the particular branch of the Christian Church of
which I am a proffessing member,—I always hope they belong to Christ, and
thus feel satisfied, although I may differ from them in some *trifling points.*—

September 24

At this gloomy season, my mind seems even more solemnized than
ever,—sickness and mortality call for serious thought.—a Death in this Village
has lately occur'd after only a few days illness, and much sickness prevails
here—and yet the gay, unthinking ones of the place are still regardless of their
latter end.—oh, that I had the eloquence of an angel that I might persuaide all
intelligent beings to come unto God! so might I be made the happy instrument of
enlightening the darken'd mind, and bringing the benighted soul to a knowledge
of that blessed Saviour who permited his own precious blood to flow in crimson
currents for the redemption of a guilty world.—I would point them to the
Spotless Lamb of God that taketh away the Sin of the World. I would say,
behold him in the Garden of Gethsemene,—behold a God agonizing for the sins
of a fallen race, until his lovely temples are bathed with drops of bloody
sweat.—agonized in body, and in spirit, and retired apart from every human eye,
and every earthly friend, he bears the heavy burden of thy sins.—he, that
Spotless One, who knew no sin himself.—at the sol[...]

[Discourse on Calvary][60]

{....} midnight hour, he sorrows all alone for thee.—yes, thy sins have wrought this agony!—Now follow him to the Pala[ce] of Caiaphas, and the Judgement hall of Pilate,—hear him insulted by the rude scoffings of the multitude, who hail him with mock hosannas on his way.—see how his friends desert him!—behold him left alone in the hands of his merciless enemies, not one pitying look to cheer him! not one relenting visage!—hear them condemn the innocent, and sentence him in whom they could find no guilt, to an ignominious death upon the cross!—behold him bearing that heavy cross to the summit of mount Calvary!—and will they crucify the Lord of Glory?—for thee, oh sinner, it is permitted!—Jesus, the spotless Lamb!—behold him nail'd upon the Cross for thee.—think how great the magnitude of thy sins, since none but so rich, so precious an attonement could suffice.—See the nails driven through his hands and feet!—Behold the crimson current flowing from his side!—oh! I would ask each child of Adam, if they could behold unmoved a Saviour's sufferings.—A Saviour Crucified for them!—Yes, miserable sinners that we are!—*Our* sins, they peirced the lovely Saviour's hands, and feet, and side!—it was *our* sins that caused that precious blood to stream from the brow of Calvary!—for we have *all* sin'd, and gone out of the way.—there are none righteous.—*all* have transgress'd the *Law*.—and *all* have come under condemnation *by the Law*.—but thanks be to the Lord who hath made a way for our escape, and freely given his only Son to suffer death upon the Cross, that we rebellious mortals might be liberated,—that we might be ransom'd from everlasting death, and misery,—the ransom is paid which redeems us from the curse of the Law!—Jesus hath paid the price, and given Victory over sin, and Death, and the Grave!—through *his* merits, and sufferings, he offers everlasting Life,—an Eternity of happiness!—he bids us believe, repent, and live.—Then let us look to him, and bless the great, the attoning sacrifice, which sets us free from sin, and Death Eternal—Lovely, glorious plan of Salvation!—why cannot *all* see the beauty of its consistency in its every part?—I would that I had an Angel's eloquence, and that the spirit of the Lord was on me to speak! then might I without presumption say [to] sinners round.—I "pray you in Christ's stead, be ye reconciled to God." [...] I would say, and "kneel before the Cross, and like another Magdalene {....}

---

[60] At this point in the diary there is an extended discourse on themes related to Calvary. Since there is a break in the order and the dates cannot be confirmed, I have chosen to separate this lengthy theological reflection under its own heading.

[...ated] in them—it would seem quite a strange thing that [...] ever in their
speech wound each others feelings,—and if [...] err, and through mistake offend,
it would be well for the others, [to have] the power of that forbearance so
necessary in the cause in which [we] have *all* embark'd, lest the insulted spirit of
God should take its [power] forever from Port Royal, and Infidels boast, and the
daughters of Zion mourn.—Yet stay, insulted spirit stay!—and manifest to
sinners round, how good, and lovely a thing it is for "Brethren to dwell together
in unity."—let them admire the beauty, and consistency of the Christian plan in
its every part, whilst they exclaim—Behold how these Christians love one
another!"—Yet stay, insulted spirit and rest on him who shall next come the
holy messenger of Zion's God,—breathe thy sacred influence o'er him, and
teach him with the eloquence [of] angels, to tell over again the story of God's
redeeming Love.—let him choose *a glorious theme*, that all may wonder and
adore! that every heart may be melted into Love!—so may all dissentions, and
all rivals [...] Church's be swallow'd up in the *pure Love of God*, who for [...]
fallen race, sent his only begotten Son, cloath'd in the [flesh..] [...] nature upon
him to save from sin, and everlasting [...] who [...] his bitter enemies—oh, teach
the holy [...] tell how the Saviour of the World, condescended to [...] sorrows,
that he might bear the heavy burden of [our] sins, [he] who knew no sin himself,
but was the *spotless Lamb of* [God]—tell how the Garden of Gethsememe
witness'd his [...]—te[ll of] his meekness, and uncomplaining suffering in the
Palace of [Caiaphas] and the judgement hall of Pilate, while he only heard
around him the rudeness, and revilings of his enemies—tell how he though
innocent was condemn'd to the most shameful death,—even death upon the
Cross, and how he had to bear that heavy Cross to the summit of Mount
Calvary, amidst the insulting scoffings of the multitude, who hail'd him with
mock hosannas on his way.—then holy Spirit, inspire the messenger of Israel's
God, to tell of the last tragic scene which completed the precious sacrifice,—tell
how the Saviour of the World,—the Lamb of God, was offer'd up as an
attonement, a sacrifice for Sin!—tell how on Calvary the spotless victim bled.—
his hands, his feet, his side were [pierced]—tell how the bleeding sacrifice,
when all was done,—exclaim'd "[It] is finish'd," and bow'd his head, and gave
up the Ghost."—how the *Third* day concluded the Glorious work of
Redemption, and the Prince of Peace, even the Son of God, ascended in all his
majesty and beauty far above the heavens, to set down forever at his Father's
right hand and plead the cause of those who had rebel'd against him.—yea, let
him tell how the *Second* in the *Godhead*, came to earth, and died, a {....} that the
sacrifice was not in vain! and while I strive to make my [perf]ection sure, let

Faith assure me that the tears and prayers of penetence are received, and that the blood of a dying Redeemer hath ransom'd me.— I once thought that not having any of what I supposed very *great* offences to account for, I might rest easy, and satisfied, not percieving that the sins and transgressions every day commited were so many blemish's to deform the picture, and not reflecting that there [was] a just God of "purer eyes than to behold iniquity" however triffling I might suppose my transgressions to be.—Alas, how criminal has [been] this security! and how much should I dread the frown of an angry [God] were it not for the merits of that blessed Saviour in whose mediation [I] trust.—yes, I hope, and rejoice in the hope that his mediation [will] one day be exerted in my favor!— my mind expands at the thought!—my soul is lifted up by the elevating idea!— eleva[ting] indeed!—for oh how delightful to suppose, that the time may [come] when through the imputed righteousness of that divine intercessor I [may] be admited into the society of the blessed, wise as angels, with the simplicity of children.—then shall the veil be withdrawn, and I shall no longer "see through a glass darkly,"—but what now appears incomprehensible shall be fully made known.—and hail'd by kindred spirits, and reunited to departed friends I shall seek the bosom of my God, and Saviour, and view the splendours that surround the Throne—Then shall all tears be wiped away, for all will be peace and harmony, in those blissful scenes where universal love unbounded reigns, and wreaths of glory crown immortal Life.—Judith Lomax

October 17

Have been to a Baptist Meeting,—an association I believe they term it.—I enjoy'd myself much.—good preaching and much order.—oh, it is sweet to mix with the dear people of God! and it is of little moment what they are call'd *so that they be but of Christ*.—I have just return'd from spending three days most delightfuly on the other side of the Rappahannock,—sometimes under the shelter of venerable oaks, near my favorite little Meeting House, where I oft-times spent some happy hours, now past, and gone.—and sometimes injoying myself in religious converse with dear Christian friends in the hospitable dwelling of Mr. Turner.—Yes I have found much delight, and I hope some profit, in mixing with the Baptists at their meeting under the Oaks, and in associating with dear Christian friends, at Mr. Turner's.—My heavenly Father I thank thee for all they benefits to *me*, thy poor unworthy Servant, for it is from *thy* inexhaustless treasure that I draw endless pleasures in.—it is from the fountain of Christ's love, that the love of God's dear People flow.—and it is from the same dear fountain that I derive a peace of mind "which passeth all

understanding," a peace which nothing on earth can take away, since it is the gift
of a Saviour God,—my Redeemer gave it! and he purchased the gift for me with
the rich drops of his own precious blood which he shed for many.—Yes, I feel
that I can use the words of a Job of old.—I can exclaim that "my Redeemer
liveth."—and when by his blood my Soul was ransom'd, I received, from him
that peace which nothing here on earth can rob me of,—even "a Peace which
passeth all understanding."

October 20

Have just return'd from the house of Mourning—the destroying angel has
been abroad, and smitten *one*, even the Head of a *family*—the *Husband*, the
Father, is gone! gone to that "bourne from which no traveler returneth."—
Awful event! on Thursday evening, I beheld Doc.t Tenant expiring, the shades
of death were closing fast upon him,—his family wept around,—my heart bled
for *them*, for *him*,—yes, my trembling heart throb'd, it bled at every pore for
her, the *dear* afflicted widow, and the helpless orphans.—and alas! for *him*—ah
me! poor Tenant!—whither has the fleeting spirit fled?—yesterday I beheld the
lifeless remains of Doct. T.—of him who shone conspicuous in the brilliant
circle,—Taste, and talents were his!—but what availeth it?—Ah me! my
heavenly Father! my divine Master! my Saviour, my mediator! on thee I call!—I
have just return'd from the house of Mourning,—I have beheld the livid
countenance of Death.—My God behold me awe-struck in thy presence,—and
while I bend before thee this night, imploring thee for more grace, for more
holiness, oh, hear thy supplicating child!—fit me for thy kingdom,—oh, sanctify
me wholly.—complete thy work.—purify my heart from every earthly alloy.—
let me at the last be found so pure,—so holy, so that I may gain admittance into
thy heavenly mansions, and be worthy of associating with the holy band that
surround thy throne rejoicing,—Heavenly Father! I would be thine intirely.—I
give myself to thee,—'tis all that I can do. Jesus my all!

[No Date]

Mr. Wydown spent two, or three days with me, surely it was God who
directed him to our Village, and to my abode! his Sermons, and his lessons of
wisdom, shall be treasured in my remembrance.—methinks I hear the Reverend
Man of God, giving me sage advice, and lessons of instruction.—yes, Wydown,
thou who hast buffeted the storms of Life! I will remember all thy councils, all
thy excellent advice! —thou who hast known adversity, hath councel'd me, and
I will remember all thy lessons, for adversity, is the school of Virtue, and the

school of wisdom.—I will remember the sorrowful tale of thy worldly misfortunes,—but I will not call thee, unfortunate, I better love to call thee, *the Man of God*.—for what are all the trials, and temptations of this transitory life, when we have *eternity* in view?—Smith has gone on a long expidition, he has promised me a Letter,—God deals very graciously by me, in giving me *Christian friends*, I find the *spiritual* tie a very binding one,—sweet are the friendships form'd in Christ!—

A few evenings since, I made a new Christian acquaintance. Mr. Belknap, introduced to me by Mr. Turner,—a spiritual Man I am convinced he is! he was a classmate with my favorite Andrus, whose worth he loves, and estimates, no wonder then, that it feel myself much his friend.—The Rev. Mr. Belknap appears to be truly a Man of God.

October 28

Have met with a disappointment I not being able to get on to a meeting 15 Miles below this.—a meeting of Episcopal Ministers, from whose preaching I anticipated much profit, and expected to have been highly gratified,—but it is all for the best, and I am well convinced that disappointments are not unfrequently beneficial to us.—they serve methinks to humble our proud rebellious spirits, and make us to feel our dependance on that great and omnipotent Being who deals out our portions in due season.—As for me, a poor needy worm of the dust, who every day feel my own imperfect state, it is good I am convinced that I should be kept low in comforts.—my God sees fit that it should be so, were it otherwise, I might perhaps acquire spiritual pride, be vainly puff'd up, and forget how very weak and insufficient a being I am.—rather than it should be so, keep me still my heavenly Father humbled low at the foot-stool of thy power, there let me look to Jesus, the divine mediator! from whom cometh every good and perfect gift.—and while I own him as the great high Priest, the rich attoning sacrifice, let me from his fountain, drink endless pleasures in.—Give me to partake of his meek, and lowly spirit.—so may I be ever kept from murmuring, and repining at his all wise dispensations.—and so shall I ever enjoy that peace of mind which passeth all understanding.—Jesus thou great Bishop and Shepherd of Souls! it is thou alone who knowest what is good for me, for thou art the wisest, and the best!—keep me, oh keep me ever thine!—shadow me with thine almighty wings, and let me be still found waiting at thy feet, til all thy will be done.—

{....}again feel that the love of God, a wish to serve him, [preeminent] in my mind,—My Saviour God, fills every avenue of my heart.—Then let me be content, and ever trust in thee my lord, "Sweetly waiting at thy feet, till all thy will be done."—

Sabbath Morn

I have been looking over my last exercise commited to this sheet, and the blush of shame mantles my cheek, to find in it something like a murmuring spirit something like a disgust for Life,—oh, let me guard against a repining spirit! let me not be ungratefuly remindful of the numberless blessings daily shower'd upon me by the bountiful hand of a merciful, and omnipotent Father in heaven.—My Life is quite a happy one, at least I think so, when I compare it with the Lot of many,—oh, surely I ought to be happy, and ought to be very thankful, when I remember all that a God, a redeeming Saviour, has done for me,—think of how the Lord has dealt with me, a poor unworthy worm of the dust.—how "he has raised me out of the mire and pit," and placed my feet on a rock,—how he has given me not only temporal comforts, but greater still, spiritual ones, that I trust shall last forever, even when all that is temporal, shall crumble in decay.—oh! when I think of these things, when I think of all his marvelous great kindness, to one who has been unworthy of even his slightest blessing, I feel ready to exclaim in the words of the Psalmist,—"Praise the Lord, oh my soul, and all that is within me, praise his holy name."—But an indulged child, tho it may be very happy while traveling, and wandering abroad, yet will it sometimes think of the home of its Father, will sometimes feel a longing desire to be there, not so much, that it feels weary of its pilgrimage, but in the affection of its heart, it sighs to behold the beaming countenance of a fond Parent, to bask forever in the sun-shine of his presence, and in [so] blest a home, to feel safely shelter'd from every storm!

"Vanish then this world of shadows,
 Pass the former things away;
Lord appear! appear to glad us,
With the dawn of endless day.
O conclude this mortal story;
Throw the universe aside;
Come eternal King of glory,
Now descend—and take thy Bride."

—On Thursday our Venerable Bishop will preach here—[grac]ious is God in sending his chosen servants to this rebell[ious] Village!—oh! why are the People like the deaf Adder that stoppeth her ears, which refuseth to hear the voice of the charmer, charm [...] never so wisely?"—I had thought the *dear*

Episcopal had intirely given us up,—that they had beheld the Village, that they all thought "there was not *one* righteous,—no *not one*." and that they had one, and *all* deserted us *forever*.—and now lo! here comes the very head of the Church.—oh, that his visit may be blest!—It glads my heart to think of his coming!—How the Christian delights to taste of the celestial fountain!—and how having once tasted we thirst for more,—again we thirst,—deeper, and deeper we drink, and still the stream flows on, purer, and more pure, fraught with Nepenthean virtue.

Thursday Morn

Visited on her deathbed the oldest inhabitant of this Village, the dews of death were on her, she was dying fast, but whilst I held her clammy hand, she cast on me an affectionate look, she seem'd truly happy, and addressing me by name, observed, that tho it was hard for the body and soul to part, yet it was a blessed thing to go to Jesus, that she felt she should soon be with him, her countenance was expressive of resignation and triumphant joy.—"Blessed are they who die in the Lord!"—I was call'd from her bed-side to see our dear Bishop, who had just arrived in the Village, I follow'd him to the Sanctuary of God, and heard him deliver an excellent Sermon, his subject was the 3d chapt. of the Gospel of St. John, beginning at the 14th Verse.—"And as Moses lifted up the Serpent in the Wilderness etc.."—oh, it was a glorious Sermon!

Saturday Eve

Have assisted in puting into her last narrow house, the old Lady mention'd above, she died on Thursday night,—oh, it was an awful thing, to feel the cold, dead weight of a lifeless Body!—all night I thought of it,—and yet the inanimate clay, wore such a look of happiness, that Death seem'd lovely.—Oh Death! it is for our good, sometimes to behold thee, to become familiarized to thee, and to remember, that we who yet survive, will one day, (and how [long] we know not) be clasp'd in thy cold embrace.

November 28

Have [...] return'd from a most delightful visit to King George County, [heard] three more discourses from the dear, excellent Bishop, all of [them] good and melting the heart to good,—oh, how highly favor'd [...]—may all that I have heard from Bishop More, both in and out of the Pulpit, be sanctified to me!—two days did I spend with him at Mr. George Johnson's enjoying the privilege of spiritual conversation, such days, such hours, are not to be effaced from my remembrance,—Ever will I remember my dear spiritual Father, and the beloved pious People of King George County! oh! it was sweetly gratifying to every feeling of my sensitive mind, after the divine service of the day, and the excellent sermon was over; to feel my hand alternately grasp'd by my beloved Mrs. Mason and dear Anne Yates, introducing me to all their pious Friends,— Thus have I found friends in the People of God!—But it is to the *great first cause* that I owe it all, it is from the inexhaustable fountain of Christ's love, that the love of his people spring,—and "Lord! what am I, that thou art thus mindful of me?"—But "continue forth thy loving kindness," and let us the people of thy care, continue to love on, while here on earth, and at the last, be brought in a holy, and united band, united in Christ, to dwell forevermore in his presence, in the heaven, of heavens, where there is Life, and joy, and Love forevermore.— The Bishop return'd with me to the Village, and comply'd with the request I was commission'd to make to him, namely to perform the burial service over the Grave of the deceased old Lady, who had been a member of our Church.

December 1

Have commenced making some improvements in my habitation, puting a new inclosure, etc.—my mind has been much exercised by it,—whether might not the money I shall bestow on it, have been better appropriated by giving to the poor, and in aiding with it religious institutions?—but then I have comfort in thinking that the workman who I imploy is a poor Man with a family, the money will be the reward of the industry of an indigent Man, who wants it,—The new inclosure will secure me from depredations on my little property, so that I can in leisure moments indulge myself in cultivating my plants etc.. and seeing them bloom beneath my fostering care.—oh, how I love to behold the power of God exemplified through all his works! I love to watch the growth of vegetation, and mark how his glory shines in the expanding of even an infant bud!—I am the most domestic animal alive,—I can love the rose that entwines itself at my window,—The tree that shades my dwelling,—and [the] Violet that breathes its perfume around it, as tho they were objects warm'd by Vitality, for in the affection of my heart, I exclaim,—"my Father made them all!" and I seem to have a love for all, both animate, and inanimate, that my heavenly Father has created.—I adore him through all his works!—I value all his gifts and the many comforts with which he has bless'd me.—and in the morning when I awake up after refreshing slumbers, I bless him for it, and am thankful for the downy couch on which I have reposed, and dreampt of happiness—it is sweet to be a Christian, and to feel the love of God pervading every avenue of the heart.—

December 17

The day had closed in, it was dark and cold, and the rain and hail, beat against my little habitation,—I had dismiss'd my work, and books, and sat musing all alone by the fire-side; when a loud rap at the door, announced a visitor,—it was the husband of my friend Harriet, who call'd on me with a Letter from his Wife—how unexpected was the pleasure! we spent some delightful moments by my fire-side,—and then he left me, to fulfill an engagement to lodge else-where, promising me to call in the morning for an answer to the letter,—again this morning he has been with me, we have taken a social breakfast together, and I have made him the bearer of my answer to his Wife.—How gracious is God in giving me friends amongst the people of his love!

December 25 ["Natal Day"—Christmas 1820]

Glorious Epoch!—The Nativity of a Saviour!—may he have lived and died for me!—this day I feel his heavenly presence, this day I feel him in my heart, he fills every avenue of it.—Why is it that clouds and darkness some times shadow my mind, excluding from it the irradiating beams of love and hope? why am I sometimes the victim of doubt respecting my own situation?—away with these fearful foreboding! it is the work of Satan, he seeks to intimidate me, and shake my faith.—When I search my thoughts, my secret wish's, I feel the sacred witness there, feel that I can be none other than the Child of God, born of his spirit!—surely our God in this our time, seldom acts on the mind by miraculous signs.—his word lies before me,—with his grace, let me endeavour to act up to what it teach's, let me endeavour to imitate the bright example set us by a redeeming God, while he wander'd here on earth, taking upon him for our sakes, suffering humanity, yes for us, a God deign'd to descend on earth, and cloathed himself in the sufferings of the flesh,—for our sakes he became a Man of sorrows, and was acquainted with grief.—and shall I then who rank myself amongst his followers? shall I then doubt his mercy, and compassion towards me for whom he bled and died?—oh let me doubt no more, while I every day feel renewals of his grace, bearing me up in this world of sorrow.—surely, I am the Child of his love, and the attoning blood has not flow'd in vain!—he is rich in mercy, and abundant in grace, and will perform all his promises,—may his happy influences so *sanctify* my *heart*, so *purify* my *will*, that I may *will* to do his perfect law in holiness,—oh, may I with his divine grace directing me, endeavour to track his footsteps, and pursue after righteousness—may he implant in my heart, a remembrance of his deep

humility.   remember how he bore the false accusations, the bitter revilings of
his enemies, their scoffs, their brutal jests.—but the hardest blow was yet to
come, because it was to be inflicted *by those he loved*; *deep* rankles the wound
inflicted by *those we love*!—but in *this*, as in every other way, he has shown us
how to suffer—it was *him* who [hath] permited the treacherous kiss, sealing the
falshood of one proffessing friend.—another denied him, and all forsook him,—
and yet he meekly bore it,—crying, "Father not my will, but thine be done!"—
oh let me treasure these things in my mind! let me endeavour to imitate them,
and follow after righteousness!—so shall I "be with him in parradise," I shall be
with him even at the right hand of his Father, and be hail'd by kindred spirits in
a purer sky.—I sometimes *do* hope that I love God supremely,—at this time on
the natal day of a dear Redeemer, methinks he fills my heart intire.—Absented
from all my Relations, and not one person near, who feels any peculiar interest
in me, I seem to stand alone in this wide world, as if on earth I had none, no
none, to care for me—no not one,—but when I glance my eyes from earth to
heaven and view my Saviour there, beholding him as the friend of the friendless,
and the Father of the Fatherless. I then feel a happy assurance that *there is one*
who careth for me, one who marks my goings out, and my comings in, and who
is I trust about my path, and about my bed, who spies out all my ways, who
keeps me as the Apple of his eye, and who I trust will never forsake me!—oh
may he have been born for me!—may he have lived for me, and may he have
died for me!—and at the last may I come to his eternal joy, never to sin or
sorrow more—hail'd by kindred spirits in a purer sky, oh my I hear the joyful
[cry] of "come, ye blessed of my Father, inherit the crown prepared for {....}"

> No foes invade this happy place,
> Where the Redeemer reigns on high.
> Where Friendship smites on ev'ry face,
> And sparkling beams in ev'ry eye.
>
> But O! for those who love the Lord,
> His own unchanging word declares;
> No eye hath seen, or ear hath heard,
> Nor heart conceived what he prepares.
>
> And now may *I* by saving grace,
> Still persevere unto the end;
> So may I win this heav'nly race,

And to my Father's Courts ascend!

There may I swell the grateful song,
Which sweetly shall free grace repeat;
Be one the blessed Saints among,
And worship ever at his feet.

This Hope shall cheer my latest breath,
So thro' my Saviour shall I brave
That last dread Foe!—insatiate *Death*!
And *Shout Victorious O'er The Grave!*

December 30

The Presbyterian Brother has again preach'd to us, and to my great mortification, from having had no notice of his preaching, I was not in the Church at the commencement of his discourse, but what I heard of it, was very *great*, and very *appropriate*, for it was an affecting warning to perishing sinners.—oh that Port Royal would yet be wise, ere a sudden destruction come unawares upon the Village!—By getting too late to the Church, I lost the Text, but readily supposed from the tenor of the Sermon, that it was from the parable of the Ten Virgins.—Surely, if the Preacher observed *me* entering the Church so late, he must have concluded that *I* at least, was one of the five unwise ones.— but he would not have judged me by *this*, could he have *known* the *real state* of the *case*.—for I was in readiness in one moment after I heard there was preaching at the Church.—my Bonnet and Shawl soon went on, and I swiftly *ran* to the sanctuary of my God.—How strange it is, that both times the Rev. Presbyterian has preach'd here, I have received no notice!—Well, he has himself now, given notice from the Pulpit that he will preach here again the Sabbath after next, and with the divine blessing I trust that then at least, I shall not be found amongst the unwise, and slothful Virgins.—There is somewhat peculiary interesting in the preaching of this Presbyterian Brother and I am anticipating a rich Gospel feast, in hearing him again.

•1820•

January 13

I have not been disappointed! the Rev. Mr. D. has again preached on the Lord's day—I was determined to be in readiness to drink in all from the precious fountain of Christ's love, through one who appears to be a faithful ambassador, I was *this* time in Church before the Minister, and I believe lost not one word of his excellent discourse.—His Text was from the first Epistle of Peter,—first Chapter,—and twenty second Verse—"See that ye love one another with a pure heart fervently."—And well did he inforce the subject of Christian Charity!—methinks this Presbyterian, beautifuly chooses his subjects, and suits them well to this sinful Village.—Though not a member of the particular branch of the Christian Church to which he is attach'd, yet do I sincerely wish him well in his endeavours to do good here.—may the cause of the Lord prosper!—no matter for *Name*, so that the *primitive* one of *Christian* is retain'd.—oh, that *some* in this place, who *profess* to be of Christ, would profit by this last discourse!—may the Lord open their minds to *a real* knowledge of *Christian Charity*!—Little did the Preacher think, while he beautifuly pursued his subject, that there was one *persecuted Episcopalian* in the congregation, who thank'd him, next to God, for every word he utter'd.—when the Preachers preach well, it would be good for us to give to *God*, the glory.—How much do I delight in listening, when the Preachers choose some of my favorite themes!—such as the Love of God.—Christian Charity,—Holiness of Heart, etc, etc.—it is then my charm'd attention hangs on every word they utter.—but let me give to God the Glory.—and oh what reason have I to glorify his name, and every day to acknowledge his transcendent goodness to me his poor unworthy Creature!—What a lonely and desolate Being, should I be in Port Royal, where I meet with no according mind.—no associating spirit, were it not for the endowments with which he has enrich'd me!—and that *best* one of all, his own *free Grace*.—Surely then I have; I feel that I Have, a kind indulgent Father!—a faithful, and benevolent Friend even "*Our* Father who art in Heaven."—and oh, that he may continue the songs of Redeeming love!

March 3

Received the wish'd for letter from Mr. W. informing me to whom I should inclose my Subscription payment, for the missionary institution, pleased am I, that I can now send it on.—But still no Repertory,[61] this is strange! every post-day I feel disappointed in not receiving the expected numbers, but disappointments are good for me, they serve to humble me,—in all things I see the goodness of God exemplified towards me.—and in all things, I will bless his name.

(Tuesday Morn)

Have just sent my Mite of 5$ to the missionary institution, may it be bless'd!—and may my heavenly Father enable me to enlarge my Subscription hereafter!

(Tuesday Morn)

Have again been favor'd by hearing the sound of the gospel from the lips of the Rev.d Mr. Brice, of the Baptist Church.—I hope his excellent discourses will prove profitable to me.—Have become somewhat acquainted with him, he has shown a friendly interest in my soul's salvation, for which I thank him.—he has left us now, perhaps never to visit us again, but in heaven I trust, we Christians of every denomination shall meet,—yes, we shall all meet there in one holy band of love, and crown'd with wreaths of glory, sing the praises of our redeeming God around the blood wash'd throne forever.

March 26

My Baptist Friends are exemplifying their love towards me, by endeavouring to persuade me to unite myself to their Church,—I gratefully feel the well meant endeavours of this respectable body of Christians, for I am very sure that their solicitations, spring from the fountain of Christ's love.—they think immersion necessary, because they have no faith in Infant Baptism, and they wish moreover, to have me more closely united to themselves,—for all this I thank them, but feel that my Episcopal opinions, and sentiments, can never be

---

[61]The *Washington Theological Repertory* is an evangelical, Episcopalian journal published in the area of Washington city during these years. Apparently Judith Lomax was on the subscription list for this journal, the first issue of which was distributed in August of 1819. An extant copy of the entire series is in the holdings of the Virginia Theological Seminary Library, Alexandria, Virginia (the same institution to which Lomax made contributions, as it was founded officially in 1823). *The Repertory* has been quite helpful in terms of setting the stage for Lomax's life, since we can assume she was reading this publication with some regularity. Mr. W may refer to Rev. Wydown, an Episcopal clergyperson, to whom she refers directly again at several points later in the journal.

relinquish'd. having according to my belief, received "the outward, and visible sign" once, I dare not receive it again, for where is the Scripture for a second Baptism by water.—Yes, I trust I have received "the outward and visible sign" *once*, and that in the name of the Father, and of the Son, and of the Holy Ghost, I have been permited the privileges of Christian fellowship, and ultimately received the inward, and spiritual grace, by that *only second* baptism; the renewal of the heart, by Fire and the Holy Ghost.—Thus am I seal'd, as I trust the Child of God, and a joint heir of the covenant of Grace.—but oh, my heavenly Father! should I be deceived in this, I pray thee thy grace to impart, and shew me that better way.—thou knowest my desire towards thee.—thou knowest that I would fulfil all thy will, even in the least little, and it is the *fear of adding* to thy word, that withholds me a second time from the Water,—could a conviction be brought home to my mind that I had never been Baptised, that the command of God had never been fulfiled in me,—*then, and then only*, would I receive the ordinance by immersion!

The Baptists are a truly spiritual people, and I feel myself united to them in the bonds of Christ's love, and Christian fellowship.—they are pleased to call me *Sister*, and most highly do I prize the dear affinity!—Heavenly Father! fit me for thy Kingdom.

March 30

Have again visited the House of mourning and beheld the awful spectacle of Death.—The lovely Mrs. C—on whose youthful cheek, the roses shed their brightest bloom. now lies cold and inanimate in the narrow house; and consign'd to kindred dust.—Last night by the glimmering light of the Candle, I beheld that pallid countenance, which only a few short weeks ago, was irradiated by youthful beauty;—even in Death it was lovely, it wore so sweet, so serene an aspect. that while we gazed on it, we might have immagin'd, she but sweetly slept, but that the breathing was not there.—It is about 4 weeks, and a few days, since the lovely Mrs. C.—became the delighted Mother of a beautiful Infant, she had been only 12 months the Wife of an affectionate Husband, when the thread of Life was cut.—She was thoughtless of Death,—the blow was sudden!—what an awful lesson!—Only a few weeks back, and Mrs. C, was blooming in loveliness!—caress'd by her friends!—Wealth, and Happiness, opening to her view!—What is she now?—Alas! cold and insensible;—the clay cold sod covers her narrow dwelling!—ah, me!—"Does youth, does beauty read the line?" {....} order all things well? for is not this a probationary state? and are we not here upon trial?—*who are we* that we should reply to God, and sketch out our own plans?—he who rulest the spheres, and orders all things for the best, knows better than we do ourselves, what is good for us, and it is downright rebellion in us to form out our own visionary plans, even though we may think that they center in good, and in the love of God,—how many devices has Satan to delude the heart of the Christian! but God will not let it be, and in tender mercy he often disappoints our plans, that he may teach us a knowledge of himself, and that he is the *only true good*, he claims our hearts *entire*, and binds us to him with the cords of love, he gives us that peace which the world cannot give, and he has promised that he will never leave us nor forsake us,—*all,— all* may change, yet will *he never*.—the Sun, the Moon, the Stars, shall fade away, this Globe shall crumble into atoms, yet will his promises remain, they will be fulfill'd to the Christian, and exceeding great, and precious promises they are!—then oh my Lord! my Savior! and my God!

> "The dearest idol I have known,
> Whate'er that idol be;
> Help me to tear it from thy throne,
> And worship only thee."

Oh, my heavenly Father, make me all thine own!

Judith Lomax

Saturday, May 6

Heard this day an excellent discourse from one of the Methodist brethren, Mr. C., his text the 7th verse of the 2nd chapter of Zachariah, "Who art thou oh great mountain? before Zerubbabel, thou shalt become a plain."—my heart felt much refresh'd by the discourse, there was much comfort in it to the believer; Mr. C. permitted me to remain in the class, he exhorted me delightfully, bid me press on, and every difficulty impeding the Christian course would be removed or disregarded—oh! at that moment I felt a heavenly calm diffused over my mind I felt "that peace which passeth all understanding," and which the world can neither give, nor take away—I felt what it was to be a Christian!—J.L.

Sabbath Day, May 14

On this, the Lord's holy day, I have heard a very spiritual discourse from one of the Baptist brethren Mr. M—he spoke beautifuly of the communication between God and the Christian, of wing'd seraphs who were continualy speeding backwards, and forward. My mind was elevated, in the moment, I almost fancy'd I could hear the rustling of their wings as they hover'd near me, ready to catch the thought, the prayer of my heart, and bear it to the throne of

Grace.—oh how ought I to rejoice when my Lord and, my God, vouchsafes his presence to me! and I feel I am not half grateful enough.—oh, my blessed Saviour! increase my desires towards thee, and make me the humble instrument in thy service, make me but a doorkeeper in the house of my God, and it will be enough.

Thursday, May 18

Received a spiritual and affecting letter from a Sister in Christ, inclosing one from Mr. — he bids me remember him, he bids me pray for him,—oh! can he ever be forgotten? *never, never*—yes, he *is* and *shall* be remembered in *every* prayer.—Christians should pray for each other.—Oh, my heavenly Father, let thy best blessings rest upon him!—and for me, oh shine upon me the light of thy reconciled countenance, and "drive these dark clouds from my mind" that now oppress it—Why should I feel dark, and cheerless, when the great "Shepherd, and Bishop of Souls" is still with me?—J.L.

May 20

Heard two very good sermons from the Methodist Brethren, I seem'd refresh'd under their preaching—oh, that every Sermon be sanctified to me.—J.L.

May 21

Have again attended the preaching of the Methodists, felt my feelings much excited, they spoke of the crucified Saviour until my heart was melted within me. I communed with them.—yes, I have again approach'd my Father's board, [...] he manifested his presence to me, and my soul was refresh'd—oh, my bleeding Saviour let thy spirit dwell within me, to light me on my way, and oh in thy infinite mercy make but the humblest instrument in thy service for I would rather be a door keeper in the house of my God, than to serve in king's palaces.

May 26

Have been writing to a dear Sister in Christ—Christians when separated, should write often, and exhort one another, as the Apostles did of old, God perhaps may sometimes use this as a means amongst many others, of keeping alive the heavenly flame in their hearts, and causing it to burn with a brighter, and purer lustre,—The Christian name is a sacred one,—oh! that *I*, that *all* who bear it, might be as burning and shining lights in the Church of Christ, to light others on their way,—so may the kindling flame like the electric fluid fly from one to one, each lighting the other, oh may it fly from pole to pole, till it reach earth's remotest verge, till the glorious contagion shall be caught by all, and the divine flame penetrate every heart!—then shall all be *one family, one fold in Christ*, and love shall be the sacred bond to unite them,—oh, how sweet the bond that love shall bind!—how sweet to sing in one general chorus the promises of Immanuel!—I love sometimes to give the reins to my imagination, to let it soar as with an Eagle's flight, and with an eagle's glance survey in anticipation that glorious epoch, now perhaps fast approaching, when every knee shall bow to the living God, and every heart, and every tongue confess the Christ,—the blessed Saviour, who made himself the sacrifice for sin, [and bled] to redeem a fallen World.—when righteousness shall cover the face of the earth, even like the waters of the great deep.—and all shall sing a new song, even a general thanksgiving unto our God.—for has he not said that "he would be a light, to lighten the Gentiles, and the glory of his people, Israel."— Christians have much to do: each one of us ought to endeavour with the grace of God, and according to our several abilities, to aid the great, the glorious cause!—how is it that our hearts are so dull? and how is it that we so often pray, ' Thy kingdom come, thy will be done on earth as it is in heaven," and yet do so little, so very little for the advancement of that kingdom?—at least I find it is so with myself,—I think that my heart's desire is with God, that I love him supremely,—but oh! surely if this were so, I should do more to serve him— nevertheless, leaning on the bosom of Jesus, I will still press on;—who knows but he may yet make me an instrument in his service, all mean and humble as I am.—he knows the secrets of all hearts, he sees into the inmost recess's of mine,—and he knows that I would rather "be a door keeper in the house of my God, than to serve in king's palaces."—I always feel myself "the bruised reed" so weak, so frail, that I need all the help of a redeeming Saviour,—but he has said, "my grace shall be sufficient for thee", and he has also said, " I will never leave thee nor forsake thee."—these are his precious promises, and they will remain forever unbroken for the Christian, for God is the same, yesterday, today, and for ever, oh, how comforting! how supporting to the Christian! it is this sure Rock [...] foundation, these blessed promises of a bleeding Saviour, that enables us as we journey on pilgrims in this vale of tears; to smile through the mist of our fears, even amidst the dark clouds that sometimes envelope us,— yes, we can smile and wonder *why* we mourn.—It is the glorious privilege of the Christian, to look beyond this vale of tears, and wait in humble submission the time, and the coming of the Lord.—then when we shall have passed through "the Valley and the shadow of death," then shall the veil be withdrawn, and we shall no longer see as through a glass darkly, but the glorious Majesty of the Lord shall be fully reveal'd for us, and what whilst here on earth had appear'd incomprehensible to us, will be fully made known.—Then shall the Christian friends who have been parted in this world of sin, and sorrow, meet again, they shall meet *to part no more*, they shall meet in Christ, they shall feel that in his presence there is fullness of joy, and peace, and life forevermore.—Oh! They shall feel, and see, and know, more than the heart whilst confined in this earthly tabernacle of clay can conceive, more than ear hath heard, or eye witness'd for the joys of heaven can be but faintly picture here;—it is enough that with the eye of faith, we can perceive that there *are* treasures laid up for the righteous, but "immagination's utmost stretch" cannot conceive their boundless magnitude.— methinks I could dwell forever on this theme, I feel a happiness in the contemplation of eternity, that I once thought I never could feel.—oh! when the disembodied soul shall soar to the mansions above, and there substantiate all its airy dreams!—"but hush, my fond heart hush."—Thought is lost in Wonder, hope, and love.

[August] 17

Heard the [...] discourse from one [of the] Brethren of my own denomination [and follow']d him in the divine [liturgy] of our Church it was indeed [...]—How delightful for [our] prayers to ascend in sweet union with [...] God, and responding with other Christians!—methinks the so [...]ted, must send up a grateful incense acceptable at the Throne [...] through the ever blessed and interceding Redeemer,—oh, he loves [...]ices of a "broken spirit! a broken and a contrite heart, O God, thou wilt not despise." and when we are thus "gather'd together in thy sight" and all offering with one accord their sacrifices of confession, praise, prayer, and thanksgiving; surely the mediating Saviour who ever liveth to make intercession for us, recieves and bears the offering to the Throne of Grace!—surely it is recieved by the triune God! by the Father, Son, and holy spirit!

Have again heard by Letter from my late Pastor, and spiritual friend; he is destin'd to labour in a distant land, and an unhealthy climate, far from his native home, and the friends to whom his worth has endear'd him, but he goes "bound in the spirit," and the Lord will I trust be with him,—yes, our Lord is merciful, and he has said, "mine own will I keep,"—again he has said "I will never leave thee nor forsake thee."—Then go Andrus,—intent upon they destin'd work, go, and fulfil all the decrees of thy Lord and Master, he shall support thee, and under his sheltering wings thou shalt be safe,—yes, even in the wilds of Africa, thou shalt be safe,—safe as in the most civilized corner of our dear land of liberty, our native America!—then go, thou benevolent one!—go preach to the benighted heathen, proclaim to Africa the glad tidings of Salvation, until the song of joy shall resound throughout the land, and all shall shout their Saviour, and their God—so shalt thou be like an Angel of light, dispeling the darkness of the land, and breaking the fetters of superstition.—Oh, may the barren desart bloom like the Rose!—and may Africa feel her freedom in the liberty of the Gospel!—and may thou my friend when all they work is o'er, when "after a long vernal day of life" thy labours of love have all come to a close,—oh mayest thou then in that awful day, [...] gently sigh out thy soul in the supporting arms of thy Saviour, and thy God, and wake to raptures in the World to come!

September 4

Heard an excellent Sermon from Mr. Thornton one of the Methodist Brethren, it was a discourse that furnish'd food for contemplation,—oh, that it might be sanctified to his hearers.

September 5

Attended the burial of my late much esteemed friend Mr. G. Turner, Mr. Thornton the officiating Minister, hi[...] from the first book of Corinthians Chapt 15, verse 55. "O death! where is thy [sting] O grave! where is thy victory?"—The Christian Virtues of [...dep]arted friend were admirable and truly portray'd while [...] favour'd in forcible [...] lesson on the surv[iving fr]iends, he spoke of the [...] who die in the Lord, and emphaticaly warn'd those [...]ing in their sins—he array'd delightfuly for the [...] of the Valued G.T. [...]th, may his prayers be he[ard ...] dear little ones!—and may his prayer for us all [...] and his discourse be sanctified to each one of us!—Oh may I die the death of the righteous! "—When I raise my thoughts to Mount Calvary, when I behold with the eye of Faith, and Love, the precious attonement bought with the rich drops of a Saviour and a God, methinks every thing in this perishable world sinks in the balance, and there is nothing worth living, or dying for, but the blessed Jesus,—oh, let me fly to him, let me be always with him, and may his arms be my resting place, and in the last trying agony of death, may they then prove to me, "as soft as downy pillows are."—"O death! where is thy sting? O grave! where is thy victory?—"The sting of death is sin, and the strength of sin is the law; But thanks be to God, which giveth us the victory, through our Lord Jesus Christ."

September 24

Have been with a friend to the house of mourning, it was heart-rending to hear the shrieks, to behold the tears, of the young, and afflicted Widow of a murder'd Man—murder'd; taken of in the midst of his course, thoughtless and careless of the things to come, murder'd in his *sins*!—His poor little Fatherless Children, stood around their almost frantic Mother, and unconscious of their loss, seem'd to wonder why she mourn'd?—it was a sight to have moved a heart of Stone, mine bled at every pore.—Oh, may such scenes be sanctified to me!

October 7th

Have been reading over again, my French tracts, and find them excellent, particularly one extracted from "La Reponse De Luther A Erasme."—It would appear from it, that Erasmus had been writing on the free agency of Man, and perhaps ascribing too much good to the effect of the freedom of the human intellect.—Luther beautifully replys to him, and clearly proves by arguments drawn from Scripture, and texts from Scripture; that the opperations of the holy spirit must first [...] sanctify, and purify the *will*, before it can produce any go[od t]hing.—Those who have felt the depravity, and original corru[ption] of their own heart, must acknowledge that Luther has T[ruth on] his side, that it is not until the Lord has been gracious [and] has by his influences changed the heart, that the *Creature* even *wills* to do what is *good*, but embued by the divine influences, [the] *Will still free to choose*, chooses "that better part, that cannot [be] taken away," for it is *God* that worketh in us, to *will* and to *do*.—and it is then that we feel a liberty derived from heaven, we feel it in the heaven born mind, and feel that it is endear'd to us, as being bought with the precious blood of a wounded Saviour! a Redeeming God! that it has been seal'd by the rich attonement!—I cannot view the influences of the holy spirit as doing away the free-agency of the Creature, methinks it is only his divine influence that makes us free, for it is then that we are given to view the truth as it is in Christ Jesus.— my favorite Cowper well express's it, when he says, "He is the freeman whom the truth makes free, and all are slaves beside."

October 11

Much sickness in the Village, two deaths, some lying very sick.—I have been round to visit the sick and the afflicted; when I beheld in one house a sick Mother calling in the delirium of Fever, for her Child that had just departed from this world, my heart melted,—In another house I have beheld a young Man in the morning of his days, writhing under the agony of bodily pain, in the last stage of Consumption, far from the Wife of his bosom, and his infant child,—I felt compassion for him, and said all I could to comfort him, I spoke to him of God's mercy toward penitent sinners of the blessedness of a Saviour if he would only *repent* and *believe*, and cast himself upon him, to remember that Jesus bled that *we* might be saved,—oh, I said all that such a poor, weak, unworthy being, as myself, could say to comfort him, and to edify him! I then with his own consent read to him, and pray'd for him, oh, may the Lord have bless'd my weak endeavours!—have promised to repeat my visits to the sick Man, if I myself am spared.—but alas! I always feel myself but a weak soldier of the cross; I fear my own unworthiness, while I am endeavouring to instruct others; even while I joy to speak of the God of my salvation.—oh! will I ever be, that all these doubts these fears of myself, will forever be removed?—Oh, my heavenly Father! If I am yet the spared monument of thy Mercy, "shew some token upon me for good," give me daily renewals of thy grace, and "drive [thy]...clouds from my mind,"—and if I find myself in health while I see sickness prevailing around me; oh let that health be dedicated to thee! let my time, *my all*, be *sanctified* to thee! let thy spirit ever hover near me giving me the witness that I am indeed worthy of enlisting in thy cause,—and let me have no care, but the care of serving thee.—Much do I think of these things, and of the awful eternity that awaits us all.—even [in] the visions of the night, when sleep has closed my weary eye-lids, even then, the thoughts that had employ'd my waking hours seem to be continued, and once in sleep, methought I heard the voice of some whispering spirit,—"Come sister, come! it said, or seem'd to say, thy place is here!"—Was a this a vision from heaven? or was it a device of Satan's, to delude me, and make me too sure of the affect of a highly wrought immagination.—I *will not trust* in *dreams*, but will daily, and nightly, pray to my God for more of his quickening power, oh, may the light of his heavenly countenance be forever shed around me, revealing always to me the path of righteousness; that I may continually walk in his ways, "for all his ways are ways of pleasantness, and all his paths are peace."—may he give me his grace to press on, even unto the end! so shall I at the last, be admited into his presence, and receive from him a crown of ever beaming glory.—may he grant this of his infinite mercy!

October 13

Why does the blush of shame mantle my cheek? and why does the tear of penitence start from my eye!—Am I the Child of God? and have I still to bemoan the unbiden the wandering thought of my heart?—but I will not be

discouraged—with the help of God, I will still press on, still will I implore him
on daily renewals of his grace, until I hope he will complete his work, and
sanctify me wholly, then shall every thought of my heart be found worthy in his
sight, for they shall dwell always, and forever, with the only object worthy of
my constant attention, they shall dwell unceasingly with the Lord of all my
wish's, all my enjoyments, center in this one, his adorable being, this triune
God!—let no meaner object dare intrude.—let me know none but Jesus
crucified,—him only who is worthy of being adored, and held in honor, him
only who is worthy of being praised, and loved throughout the countless ages of
Eternity!—
{...} his Text from the [...] Chapter of the first Epis[tle to] the Corinthians.—
second Verse—"for I determined no[...] anything among you, save Jesus Christ,
and him crucif[ied]

October 24

Heard yesterday a very good discourse from one of [the Bap]tist Brethren,
his subject was taken from the Revelations of [John] the sixth Chapt. and
seventeenth verse. "For the great day of his [...] is come and who shall be able to
stand."—ah, fearful interrogate[...] surely it is one which seems to be an awful,
and a solemn call on [...] search ourselves deligently for we do know that he
hath said even to [...] own people, he hath said, "Nevertheless, I have somewhat
against thee."—how accountable are we.—and surely such of us as profess to be
his followers, are more particularly accountable,—let none of us deceive
ourselves, and let us ever hold in remembrance, that as we have been call'd "into
the glorious liberty of the Children of God." So should we be mindful of the
debt of love we owe,—*sin* only can obliterate the remembrance of that precious
fountain which was so freely open'd [for] poor dying sinners on Mount
Calvary.—let none of us deceive our[selves] let us each day have it proved to us
by prayer, and close self-[exa]mination, that we have indeed been call'd
according to his pur[ification and let] us make "our calling, and election sure,"
by being very [...] have a single eye to God's glory, in the use of every [precious
...] commited to our charge,—than [...], there are some [...]—our invaluable
Time so oft mispent, calls loudly [...] no note of Time but from its loss."—and
ah who m[...] too, are misapplied the rich endowments of the intellectual [...] as
seeming more peculiary pertaining to the [...] methinks for a stricter account and

the more [...] precious [talent] is only loan'd us for a season here, [...] and sojourners [in a] vale of tears." [...] demands no oth[er][62]

Monday Morn

Have been planting out Grape Vines, [and] also planting out more Rose-bush's, and some more violets around my dwelling.—"*One* shall plant, and *another* shall gather."—It *may* be, that I am not to taste of the juice of the Vine, which my own hand has planted.—it *may* be, that ere it bears fruit to perfection, I may be call'd to partake of richer fruits in my Father's kingdom.—it *may* be too, that on Earth, I may never again have an opportunity of being invited to partake of the juice of the grape around my Father's board.—but oh, I trust, that the time will come, when I shall taste it new, when I shall drink it fresh, with an innumerable host, in *his Kingdom Above*, even, forever and ever!

And I have been planting out Rose-bush's too, and Violets, and Gessamine, and sweet Honey-suckle;—these things amuse me sometimes, but,—"*One* shall plant, and *another* shall gather."—It may be, that I shall not exhale the perfume of these, the sweet flowerets planted by my hand,—it *may* be, that my fostering care is not destin'd to be the means of bringing them to maturity, that ere they bud, and bloom, I shall be partaking of richer sweets above.—My Vines, and my shrubberys, which amuse me sometimes, while here on earth I journey on; may not perhaps bloom for *me*,—their lovely tints, are perhaps destin'd to meet the eye, and please the taste of *another*,—and while they scatter their perfumes around, some surviving friend, may bless me for so sweet a Legacy!—I have sometimes been surprized to hear persons say that it fill'd them with melancholy reflections to plant out, and make improvements, not knowing, from the uncertainty of human events, that they would live to enjoy their temporary labours, but methinks this is a selfish consideration.—for my part, I love to think, that even tho I may not be permited to reap the harvest of my temporal labours, yet *another* may be benefited by them.—I shall leave a sweet memorial of my taste behind,—I shall liter[ally] speaking,—Scatter roses in the path of another,—[perhaps] another shall enjoy their perfume, when the hand that planted, shall be mouldering into silent dust.—I love to think on these things, they create in me, no mournful reflections,—I love to think of the uncertainty of human events,—I love to think of the change that must one day take place, when even our clustering vines, our favorite flowerets, shall delight us no longer, when the freed spirit bursting its imprisonment of clay, shall

---

[62] This is one of several pages which has suffered significant damage.

delight in things of higher import,—when this diurnal span shall pass away, like the vapour of morning, exhaled by the beams of the Sun,—when even that "Sun itself, shall fade away,—the Star grow dim in age, and nature sink in years."— when *all* shall crumble into atoms,—when all shall be a wreck of Matter, and a crush of Worlds.—Oh, I *do* love to think on *all these things*—for the disembodied soul, soaring to heights sublime, shall view without dismay, the dissolution of all material substances.—it shall soar "to mansions in the sky," seeking scenes of far brighter glory, than any this delusive world can offer.—it shall seek the bosom of its God, and find its happiness there,—find it in the imperishable wealth of *sterling love*,—for all is Love in heaven—in heaven, no jaring, or discordant note shall find admitance,—In Heaven, all is love, and harmony, and peace!—There, in that blissful, happy place, shall Chaplets of never fading beauty bind the brow of the Sainted form,—and clustering Vines, that shall never wither,—and blooming flowerets that shall never fade, enwreath themselves around that happy, Sainted Soul, that has conquer'd the world, the flesh, and the Devil.—Yes, for *that* Soul, shall be prepared "Celestial Palms, and ever blooming flowers"!—Oh, may *I* reach that blessed, heavenly place of rest, and crown'd with immortal wreath live forever in the presence of God the Father, God the Son and God the Holy Ghost!—Ever blessed Spirit!—Three Persons, but One God!—Amen.—and Amen.

Thursday Morn

Repeated disappointments on Post-days,—no answers to my Letters!—no Theological Repertory the Numbers of that valuable papers have been stop'd to me, for the last three months; the rest of the Subscribers, who perhaps do not appreciate the paper, as highly as I do, and who have like me paid in advance, are regularly recieving their [...] what can be the meaning of this?—And no answer to a Lett[er] that [I wrote more] than a Month since to one of the Ministers of th[...], requesting to know, to whom I should pay my annual subscription to the Missionary Institution?—no answer return'd! poor me, and my little contributions unnoticed!—perhaps rejected, as things of little import!— but all this is well!—disappointments, and mortifications, come from the unerring hand of God, they teach us humility,—then let me receive in thankfulness, every dispensation of an all-wise providence;—"Praise the Lord, oh my soul, and all that is within me, praise his holy name."—In these little disappointments, I see the gracious dealings of God towards his poor unworthy creature; for besides teaching me humility, they plainly shew me, how little I am to depend on Creature comforts,—The Repertory, valuable for its Theological instruction, and its Classical elegance, and edited by the most eminent Ministers of my Church, who tho *I am unknown to, I revere* is a paper I delight much in; perhaps I have given too much time to the perusal of it.—perhaps I should not have spared so much time from my Bible,—perhaps I may sometimes have been seeking instruction from the commentarys, and observations of Mortals, (fallible like myself) when I ought to have been studying the Truth, as it flow'd from the original source, even from the fountain head of knowledge, God's own holy written Word!—That sacred Book, which contains it, lies by me,—his Law, his word, is open'd unto me,—why should I seek for farther aid!—oh then let me love my Bible, more, and more! let me treasure it! let me pray over it!—pray that my mind may every day be more open to the reception of its divine light.— so may I draw knowledge, from the source of *all* knowledge! and the Sunbeams of righteousness forever play around, and enlighten my mind! -- Yes, my heavenly Father sees fit to withdraw from me Creature Comforts, that I may look to *him* alone, he *wills* it, that I should be drawn *completely* to *him*;—and I have no *earthly* pastor,—no kind spiritual Friend, to aid me with sweet counsel, and direct me in my pursuits after holiness.—but I have a Monitor *within*, and light shines on me from *above*.—I feel that the great Bishop, and Shepherd of Souls is with me.—"the Lord is my Shepherd; therefore can I lack nothing."— The Christian's Life, though a state of Warfare, is yet a state of happiness, even in this World,—even here, our dawning is begun, for God gives his People peace of mind, which passeth all understanding;—and let what wi[...] we believe it to be guided by a never erring hand,—disappoint[ment] and mortification, are welcome to us, because we think th[...]{....}

{....}perhaps I may get first to the abodes of the blessed—..oh, I shall I trust, be a sainted Maid, to welcome thee! My once kind Pastor! I trust though we shall never meet again on earth, that we shall yet meet again in Christ, even in the presence of our heavenly Father, where Christians meet to part no more! —where every tear is dried. It is good for me to go to the House of Mourning, I bring away reflections from it, that give health to the Soul. Oh could the brilliant Beauty at the festival of St. John, who "trips it on the light fantastic toe" could the for one moment visit the Chamber of Death, would the permit herself to behold as I did the fearful object, shrouded and veiled beneath the spotless winding sheet. What a lesson of humility would be there!—how short lived the triumph of Beauty!—From the Grave methinks I hear a voice, and these the words, "Dust thou art, and to dust must thou return." —Prepare to die!—How awful the contemplation of Life, Death and Immortality!

•1821•

January 27

It was immediately on my return from the House of Mourning, that a letter from a religious friend was put into my hands, it began with this awful inquiry, "Was I prepared to meet the divine Bride-groom?"—was I prepared?—what a question!—I ask'd myself a thousand times—was I prepared? I thought of all the blame that had ever been attached to me, from my childhood, even up until now,—I thought of the censures that had recently been pass'd on me, by one, or two, who thought themselves privileged by long acquaintance to say hard things, I thought of every thing that could condemn me in the eye of an all searching and all just God—my blood ran cold—my limbs were froze with fear—[...] I feared I was a guilty thing—I thought of the fearful object veil'd with the snow-white winding sheet.—I thought of the day when this [...] would resemble the gastly {....} there is a resting place—but yet so doubtful am I of myself— so doubtful am I of all my motives in whatever I say, or do, that I am always timid, always fearful that I have not the glory of God in view—surely this must be the effect of weak faith! for if I strive to do my best, God will surely accept me, he will surely enable me to keep any lamp "ready trim'd." to be the "wise Virgin," in readiness to meet the divine Bridegroom.—How often do I mentally exclaim—"Try me oh Lord! and examine me. Seek the very ground of my heart. See if there be any way of wickedness in me, and lead me in the way everlasting." —and again I say—"Purge my Hysop, and I shall be clean, wash me, and I shall be whiter than Snow." My Father! and my God! hear the prayer of her, who seeks after holiness, who longs to be perfected, longs for complete sanctification, and who thinks her heart's desire is with God—*Salvation!*—oh how much does that word comprise!—*Salvation* how dearly hast thou been bought!—Behold that bloody stream on Calvary—and has it flow'd for me? —oh had the plenteous stream been divided into drops, and every drop to go to number every sin of mine, it would not have number'd half the sum; and yet the precious stream, the drops unnumbered have wash'd the Sinner's heart—Jesus my all!—dear Saviour! and hast thou bled for me!—oh never let me cause the stream to flow afresh—never let me crucify again my Saviour God! but all sanctified, and holy, let me have my lamp ready trim'd always burning!—so that at the second coming of the heavenly Bridegroom, I may be found the "wise Virgin," and gain admission to the heavenly mansion of peace, and love, and joy—so shall I win on buoyant step my airy way, and kindred spirits beckon me along—bearing my conquering palm, may I be a Sainted Maid to welcome some dear Christian friend {....}

Yes this mortal part may moulder away, and crumble into dust, for "dust it is, and to dust must it return."—even the pulsations of this sensitive heart must cease,—no more will it "turn to the touch of joy and woe, and turning tremble too."—ah me its throbs, its sufferings, will all be over!—how still, how cold, will it be within this senseless bosom!—Oh Death, how sure a destroyer art thou of this mortal part!—and yet "this corruptible, shall put on incorruption,"—the soul immortal as its sin, shall never die." It shall ascend to the bosom of its Father and its God! it shall dwell forever with him.—Happy millions that surround the throne! and shall I one day make one among you? Shall I like you, be perfected in holiness? completely sanctified? a happy beatified being?—oh, shall I go where sin, and sorrow is no more? where every tear is dried?—Shall I bear my conquering palm, a Sainted Maid! and welcome some dear Christian friend,—yes, my *once* kind Pastor! perhaps I may be permitted to welcome thee!—we Shall never meet again on earth, but I trust we shall "meet in Christ"—we shall meet in that bless'd abode, of "the just made perfect," where *Friendship* become *double refined*, and worth is crown'd by *Sainted Love*.

January 29—Sabbath Day

My God deals graciously with me, even now, I have been permitted a noble privilege, I have been permitted to *teach* others; I have just return'd from the Sabbath school, the only *female* teacher there, but with the grace of God, I will still press on.—I have been teaching Children of poor Mechanics, and some who have none on earth to help them;—oh, methought when I this day, as usual open'd the school with prayer, when I pray'd for the Children, for some dear absent friends, for one *far distant Missionary Man of God*, the spirit of God in a peculiar manner rested on me.—I did invoke my God with my whole heart and soul!—I heard a deep sigh near me, I hoped it came from one of the Girls, I feel particularly interested in those of my own sex—without the help of God, what poor helpless Beings are we!—but with the divine influence resting on us, working in us, to will and to do, what is it that *Woman* cannot accomplish?—I sometimes think we are the favorites of heaven.—that God chooses to exemplify his power, delights to carry on his work with the weakest instruments—and therefore it is, that he fills the heart of *Woman with the love of him*,—what were I if I did not love my God?—he who first loved me, who died in agony for me, sweating drops of blood, and treading the wine press all alone. This for sinners!—this for me!—was ever love like this!—This night I attend a prayer meeting—there are in this place, some of what are call'd the lower order, who profess themselves Christians, I frequently associate with them, because they converse with me on my favorite subject, the Love of God!—Those who compose this little society, are Baptists and Methodists, they are illiterate, and I being of another denomination, do not feel completely at home with them.—I seem to stand every way alone, in this wide world. in this little Village I am alone;—it is true there are some here, who call themselves Episcopalians, but I differ from *them*, as much as I do from the Baptists and Methodists—it is not *all* who call themselves Episcopalians, who are so; I wish they were, for if they were of the dear Episcopal, and understood and practiced our doctrines, then would the purity of our Church be proved, and those who are watching us with a jealous eye, could not then cry out against the Church as admitting Nominal Christians .—But God knows the sincerity of *some* of us—*God knows*, and *that* is enough!—at his Bar we shall all appear—*God*, not *Man* will judge.

Monday Morn

Last night at early Candlelight, attended prayer meeting—Yesterday as a sweet day with me, even from the first Dawn of day, and after the close of it,—it is customary with me to rise when the first ray of day light beams in at my Window—thus I have a long day, which I divide between my Religious duties, and my little domestic improvements.—But the Sabbath day is devoted exclusively to *my God*—the Weather has for some time been so inclement, that the Children could not until yesterday, assemble at the school, so that when they met yesterday,—they, myself, and three male teachers, it seem'd a season of refreshment to us all. We had more Children than usual, which delighted me, it look'd like progressing and it put me in fine spirits—the Day way closed with the prayer meeting.—I was so employ'd all the day, even from the beginning to the ending of it, in the service of God, that there was no time for a cloud, no not even one fleeting cloud, to shadow my mind,—it was one day of complete sun-shine!—At early Candlelight I attended the prayer meeting at the house of one of the Mechanics—besides myself, there were only Mechanics, with their wives, and Children, their Brothers, and Sisters, and except myself, all Baptists and Methodists, abut when we met, we knew no other name than Christ, we read, and pray'd and sung alternately—oh it is sweet for Christians thus to meet! thus to forget all distinctions, to [f]orget that there is any other name besides that of *Christian*!—And yet methinks I should feel a much higher grade of happiness were I in a place where I could associate with the dear Episcopal, with beings refined and intellectual like myself,—I love the poor, and what is term'd the lower order of society, I frequently find in them an honest simplicity that I revere, and when I find them the Children of my God, my heart instantly claims affinity with them, but still my soaring mind seems eager for something more,— oh my God! if this is sin, awaken thou my sleeping conscience, and give me yet to know it, let conscience with its still, soft voice, murmur to me, and with its gentle whispers tell me if it is pride of heart? if it is sin?—for oh! if it is sin, it is too surely one of my beseting ones.—I have by a rich cultivation of taste, accumulated quite a magazine of thoughts, I long sometimes to unlock the repository; to unbosom to an associating mind, that would return me two fold, what I could give.—oh, it is sweet to interchange our thoughts with a friend!— "Where thought, meets thought, reciprocaly soft, each other's pillow to divine repose."—when the speaking glance tell us, we are understood,

> —"Oh! there are looks and tones that dart,
> An instant sun-shine to the heart;
> As if the soul that minute caught,
> some treasure it through Life had sought."

But tho I love that intellectual refinement which we sometimes meet with in the polish'd circles of Life, yet still I have no wish to mix with the rich and fashionable.—how cumbrous is magnificence!—the moderate, and the middle station is the only *free* one, I would put in my claim for refinements, and luxuries, but they should be the refinements, of a purified intellect,—the luxuries of an uncostly and simple taste!—I would have my mind always progressing, that I might be the means in the hands of my divine Master, of instructing those of inferior acquirements—That I might be eloquent in the praises of redeeming love, lighting others, as well as myself,—oh, above all things, I would have Religion placed in the most distinguishing, and lovely point of view, that all might like me, behold, and love the beauty of it.—to promote the cause of the ever blessed Redeemer, should be the one great object to which all acquirements, all improvements, should tend.—For what are Talents?—what are acquirements?—what are the riches of the greatly improvable mind, unless we make them all subservient to the interest of him who gave them?—unless they are th[e] means of glorifying the great first cause!—We should in all situations hold in view the parable of the unprofitable Steward,—alas, I always fear that I am that unprofitable servant!—and God who knows my heart, knows, that it is that heart's desire to serve him.—but I am always dissatisfied with myself,—I am continually blaming myself,—sometimes I fear I am officious in doing what had better have been let alone,—and then again, I fear I have not been active enough in doing what I ought.—oh, I fear I am at best, but a weak and timid soldier of the Cross! I am at best, but an unprofitable Servant I fear!—Oh! when shall these dark shadows flee away?—when shall the clouds that sometimes fleet, and dart across my mind, when shall they disperse, and disappear for ever?—When shall I be perfected unto holiness!—when shall I be a beatified spirit, dwelling in the presence of God eternally!—When shall I Be so pure, so sanctified as to be found worthy of being admited into the presence of God, and his holy Angels!—a Sainted Maid, to welcome some dear Christian friend, who is like me—the Spouse of God!

February 1

Have just recieved by Post, the last kind notice of my Friend Mr. Andrus, "An Address From the Rev. Mr. Lowe, To The Agents And Colonists Destin'd To the Western Coast of Africa."—Andrus is gone! his name is the first on the list of Agents.—and in the last week, the Vessel so richly freighted Sail'd,—yes he is gone, the benevolent messenger of glad tidings to benighted Africa;—he has bid adieu forever to his native land!—no more shall I receive by Post, the kind memorials of his friendly regard, which ever since we parted, he has been in the habit of sending me from time to time.—sometimes a valuable Sermon,—sometimes a Missionary address,—but he is gone!—I shall see him no more, I shall hear from him no more—here on earth he has departed from me,—we shall never meet again, until we meet in the abodes of the just made perfect. He with three others, embark'd last week for Africa,—oh it is a glorious cause! and may these enlighten'd Missionarys, who joy in the God of their Salvation,—oh may they meet with success fully answerable to their most sanguine wish's!—may the God of all grace prolong their lives to much usefulness!—but he has said "mine own will I keep,"—and surely *these are his own*! for they in a most peculiar degree, manifest their love towards *him*, and towards their *neighbour*,—and thus do they obey all the laws of their divine Master, and law giver—They go, the Heralds of Love, and Peace, and joy,—they go, obeying the divine mandate, which hath said,—"go ye therefore, and teach all nations"—and oh, the precious, precious [...] am with you acc[...] even unto the end of the world.—then these will he keep,—they have [t]ruly forsaken *all* to follow him, and he will never leave them, or forsake [them]—but should he in his wise providence, (for his ways are not to be scan'd by short-sighted mortals) should he see fit to remove them,—should they share the fate of those who have just preceded them,—should they share the fate of Bacon, and his little Colony, and be cut off even in the commencement of their labours,—yet still will they be happy, for they will reach a home far happier than any this world can afford,—

even the home of their heavenly Father, where "a rest remaineth for the people of God,"—where they shall hear the joyful salutation, of "come ye blessed of my Father, inherit the kingdom prepared for you from the foundation of the world."—oh, they will receive deathless crowns of never fading beauty,—of far more dazzling lustre than ever graced the brows of the most brilliant Monarchs of this lower sphere!—methinks when I compare these heros of the Cross, with the war-like ones, of antiquity, and modern times, they rise in the comparison, beyond the power of words to express,—even the Spartan Leonidas, with his intrepid little band, whose meteor like course, has so often excited my wonder, and admiration,—even he dwindles into nothing, when compared with the Missionary Men of God, who go into heathen Lands, and rush into the midst of danger, clad in no armour, but the Christian one, of righteousness, and enlisted in no other cause, save that of the God of their salvation,—they go, not to shed the blood of their fellow men, or to spread terror, or devastation around them—but they go in peace, braving the dangers of an unhealthy climate, to break the bread of Life to perishing souls,—to be the means of grace even to those, who may rudely, and brutally assault them.—they go, not like Leonidas, to obey an imaginary oracle of a false God, but to obey the benevolent mandate, of the one only true God,—the triune God!—true, and just, and merciful, in all his dealings, *he wills it*, that all nations should be brought unto him,—they go, hoping to be the means of fulfilling *this* his heavenly will,—*theirs* is no meteor spark—no momentary flash, dazzling to confound!—but one unalterable blaze of light, on irradiating bright sun-shine, steady in its course, and [dipping] its beams around, discovering by the brightness of its lustre, the track of a Saviour, and the blood-stain'd Cross!—oh they go, like angels of light, "on gentle errands bent."—the go to scatter a light from heaven around,—they go, to be the blessed means of saving immortal souls to God.—Happy [Missionarys!]—may God's [...] blessings rest on you, and your [little C]olony!—but you are doubtless blest! for you must be heavenly born, and destin'd for the skies,—yet nevertheless, my feeble prayers shall ascend for you,—at early morning, and still at close of day, I will remember at the Throne of Grace, the rich, the precious freight, destin'd for Africa,—oh, they shall be remember'd in my every prayer!—all Christians should pray for them, and for the cause of Africa,—for it is the cause of God!

February 11

Have been much gratified in the preaching of Mr. Brice, of Richmond, one of the Baptist brethren, and a truly Evangelical Preacher, he appears highly

gifted, his language beautiful, and elegant,—I heard two Sermons from him, and
thought it *a rich "Gospel feast"* to set under the sound of his preaching,—since
hearing him Preach, I have spent some pleasant moments with him, at the house
of one of the Baptist Brethren, in the Village, where he took leave of us, and
departed,—It is sweet to associate with Christians, and to forget the brethren of
other denominations bear any other name, save that of Christ,—I must always
give a preference to Christians of *my own* denomination, and aid in every way
that I can, the institutions in my own Church.—But yet as I think, the probability
is, that I may never hear again the sound of the Gospel from an Episcopal
minister, I am determined to extract from *others* all the good I can,—we should
be always in the school of Christ, and think ourselves only babes in knowledge,
willing to learn, and endeavouring to progress in Christian attainments.—but I
trust "the Lord is my Shepherd, therefore can I lack nothing."—Oh let me
always be at the feet of Jesus!—always learning—always progressing!—{....}

Sabbath Night
    This morning arose as usual, at early dawn, and began the day with
Prayer—After a slight breakfast, used the Liturgy of my Church as is customary
with me—then attended the Sabbath school,—offer'd a prize to the Girl who
should first get through the Book of St. Matthew,—a new teacher come to assist
us, a spiritual Man, and sings delightfuly.—he took me, and one of my Baptist
friends, home with him to see his Wife, we had all of us, some spiritual
conversation together,—a happy little family, they seem'd to be,—the Husband
and Wife, both of them professors of Religion, apparently honest and
industrious,—we found the Wife with the bible by her,—a Cherub child lay
sleeping in the Cradle.—it was just such a scene as I love to admire,—Such a
scene as my fond immagination has sometimes sketch'd, when I have dreampt
of earthly happiness—but perhaps my vivid Fancy, could give the painting a
higher colouring, I would suppose that this seemingly happy Pair, were in
possession of intellectual acquirements,—a cultivated taste, etc. *these*, united
with their love of God, and their love for one another, would complete their
happiness,—but would these acquirements add to their happiness?—ah, me!—
Happy couple!—let me wish you nothing, that might interrupt your earthly
bliss!—My friend, and myself, spent some delightful moments with these
people,—an Overseer, and his Wife!—the dinner hour inform'd us, it was time
to depart.—they endeavour'd to persuade us, to spend the remainder of the day
with them, we excused ourselves for that time.—We have just met again with
them at prayer meeting, the Wife has appointed Wednesday evening for my

Friend and myself to visit them again.—if God is willing, I will go,—I love to contemplate happiness!—I love to behold it personified in a fond Couple, devoting themselves to God, going hand in hand together,—both of the same denomination of Christians—congenial in *all* things!—Our prayer meeting was a full one.—the singing excellent.—And now oh, my heavenly Father, watch over my slumbers, inspiring my dreams!—may my sleeping Fancy still breathe on my [ear..]{....} the dealings of a kind Father who will cause *all* to work together for good, to his favorite children,—we hope that "our light afflictions which are but for a moment," will be sanctified to us, and fit us for glory.—To *me* this intire resignation, this giving up of myself, to the great disposer of all events, is peculiarly beneficial.—I am by nature, the Child of feeling.—a deep sensibility almost approaching to Romance, has ever mark'd my Character, and too often perhaps, render'd me unhappy, for such Characters are generally the sport of the unfeeling.—This world, this selfish world, makes no allowance for any feelings that do not assimmilate with its own and that Being who is by nature embued with much sensibility, is eve liable to be made unhappy, by a quickness of apprehension, by lively feelings which are but too quick to receive the pointed stings of censure, and the jeers, and scoffs of Ridicule.—but when once Religion comes to the aid of us, the Children of sentiment, and feeling born; these natural feelings of the heart, are subdued, or at any rate, *chasten'd*— we give up ourselves to God; we cease to trouble ourselves much, about the things of this world.—the world with all its false representations, and deceitful illusions has glided from beneath our feet.—Heaven opens to our view,—and we are happy!

— To be an instrument in the Redeemer's cause, is all that my soul now pants for, while here on Earth,—and when at our prayer meetings in this Village; I am call'd on, to close the night, with my feeble supplications,—oh, then it is that my soul seems to rest on my quivering lip!—I would invoke blessings on the circle around me,—I would pray for my absent friend,—for my poor *needy self*, and oh—I would pray for the Ministering Servants of God, of *every* denomination, and of *every clime*,—I would pray for the whole world at large, for the whole Universe, created as it is, by the hand of Omnipotence.—I feel in the earnestness of my supplications, that I must draw down the blessings I invoke.—it is then, when I return home, and rest my head upon my pillow, that my quiet, and refreshing slumbers tell me.—I am happy!—Happy in loving God supremely!—Then blessed Jesus look on me, who am in meek submission,

> "Sweetly waiting at thy feet,
> Till all thy will be done."

May 1

Have heard with much pleasure, and I hope with some profit, the preaching of the two Methodist Brethren Peyton, and Davis, newly come, they appear to be faithful Servants of the most high God, and I trust in the hands of that God, and instruments of his power, they may effect much good in this quarter.—Heavenly Father,—spread thy Gospel!—speed thy word!—make it to take root in this Village—and oh let it spread far, and wide, until all nations bow to thy sceptre, and thy will be done on earth, as it is in heaven.—Oh, that the day may not be far distant, when righteousness shall cover the Earth, as the Seas cover the great deep!

May 12

Have return'd from visiting some dear, pious friends in King George County.—Oh how passing sweet is the endearing friendship, the sweet communion of Christians!—and more particularly so, when we are of the same denomination,—agreed upon all points!—for when we know that our sentiments, and opinions, are reciprocated, we feel a delightful freedom of conversation, that is highly gratifying to the candid, and sensible mind.—it is then we interchange our thoughts, banishing all fear of giving offence, or being misunderstood.—"As Bees mixt nectar drawn from fragrant flowers."—even so is the sweet communion of Christian friends, who worship God, in the beauty of Holiness.—I have spent ten or twelve delightful days amongst the pious members of my own Church, the dear Episcopal, in King George.—and thought my time well spent.—for we talk'd of God, and of Godly things, and much too did we talk of the dear people of God, who were absent, and who we delighted to rank in the number of our Christian friends.—much did we delight to mention the names of *Keech*, and *Andrus*.—yes, estimated worthies! you were often remember'd by us, your friends, while we held sweet converse together—and there is one of you, that on earth, we shall never behold again.—*Andrus*, thou pious, and faithful follower of the Lamb! where art thou now?—wandering in the wilds the scorching deserts of savage Africa, far from they native land! for thou hast forsaken all to follow him whom thy soul lovest, and he will be thy reward!—oh he will reward thee, [ten][fold],—yea, an hundred fold.—even now, thy Saviour's arm supports thee, his spirit guides thee, and Christian, he "will never leave thee, nor forsake thee."—then Andrus, pursue thy course, and spread the glad tidings of salvation, while we thy American Friends will continue to pray for thee, and still continue to remember all thy worth.—May we at the last, meet thee on "a Shore of better promise!"—Andrus, I remember thy last parting word!

June 27

Have again been over to King George County, and spent ten days much to my satisfaction with some of my pious friends there.—heard an excellent discourse from Mr. Wydown, a Minister of my own Church, it was sweet to me to join once again with other Christians in the excellent service of our Church, and to send up our united prayers in the sacred sanctuary, with those of a Man of God, thus worshiping the Lord "in the beauty of holiness."—

Heard two very impressive Sermons from Mr. Peyton of the Methodist Church; he is a powerful Preacher, and appears much engaged in the service of his heavenly Master, I judge him to be Eminently calculated to do good in the glorious cause.—Have just read in the News-papers of the safe arrival of the Nautilus, in Africa, with her precious freight of Agents and colonist—*Andrus* has gone into the interior of the Country, just as he mention'd to me he should, when I last saw him.—May the great Jehovah be with him, protecting him amid[st] every trial, and every danger!—The blessing of Israel's God rest on him, and on his labours!—The Agents, and the colonists, have my fervent prayers, all of them. Oh, that they may all be supported to the utmost, and that God may see fit to prolong their lives to much usefulness, [to] a cause so glorious!

September 27

Strange that I should so long have neglected my Note Book!—two whole month's have pass'd, and not one note have I made in this my book of remembrances of the passing time.—whence is this?—let me pass an examination, and ask myself honestly the question, if it has not proceeded from *indolence?*—alas, the blush that tinges my cheek too plainly answers in the affirmative—But now will I return to my long neglected Book, that I may "once again note down the gracious dealings of God with me, his poor unworthy Servant—record how he has been pleased to light my mind with the irradiations of his presence, giving me such views of his adorable perfection, as to fill my soul, and absorb my mind with boundless love of his deity.—ah! who can cease to love, that thinks on a crucified Saviour?—thinks on a meditorial Redeemer?—agonizing in the garden of Gethsemene!—bleeding on the cross!—and now every day shewing forth to his delighted followers, his marvelous dealings and his wonderful loving kindness.—"Praise the Lord, oh my soul, and all that is within me, praise his holy name."—Much preaching in the Village, and I hope to the profit of some.—but what has most delighted me is, that is has pleased my divine Master to send even one of his episcopal servants, bearing to us the message of glad tidings,—the Rev. Mr. Wydown has favor'd us lately with two most excellent Sermons, I found it sweet to listen to him with charm'd attention, while he preach'd Christian charity and enforced the necessity of the union of Christians, of every denomination.—and oh, it was with a pleasure unspeakable that I follow'd him through the Liturgy of my Church, uniting my voice with that of another dear Christian, Mr. Thomas Smith, lately baptized in the Episcopal Church.—oh it was gratifying [to] me, to entertain him, and Mr. Wydown in my own little dwelling, after the services of the Church were over!—Mr. S. is a very promising member of the Church his adult Baptism was the result I believe of the influences of the spirit directing him to the Episcopal Church—may he prove a shining member, and that is to be a shining Christian.

Sabbath Morn

Have been disappointed in collecting the [...] for the school—myself the only teacher to day. No preaching today, in the Village, have as usual been [...] at home,—have been much gratified these three last days in having a family of colour'd Females, to attend in my Room during my hours of Prayer, their own voluntary request to do so.—my little congregation consists of six respectable Girls, all Sisters, and all free. Two of them, are my hired Servants,—They kneel, when I kneel, they listen attentively when I hope the holy Book, and read to them the precious word of God.—and they join with me in singing the praises of Redeeming love.—Oh, delicious moments!—and today being Sabbath day I used the Liturgy of my Church,—my hearers were perfectly patient, and very attentive while I went through the service of the day.—methinks the highest privilege that Heaven grants us is, the privilege of improving others!—ah! who is there, that would refuse to be a Christian, could they but know one half of the delights of being a Christian?

Sabbath Night

Just return'd from associating with the Methodists, and Baptists in prayer.—we had a full meeting to night.—and many join'd us in singing to the praise, and glory of God.—And now may God send his holy angels to watch over me, and guard me from the dangers of the night!—setting bounds even in sleep, to my roving Fancy, or else causing it to ascend to heavenly thing—oh,

God of Life!—even in dreams, let my thoughts be pure,—so that sleeping, or waking, my Motto may be "Holiness unto the Lord."

Saturday Eve

This day Mr. Cook preach'd to us, his farewell Sermon,—it was an excellent one, and very affecting, he exhorted the Christians to perseverance, whilst he warn'd the careless Sinners.—May this, his last Sermon, and every one that he has ever preach'd in this place be sanctified to each one of us!—and may the blessings of God rest on him, wherever his destination may be! for I believe him to be a faithful [follower] of the Lamb.

[...]our [Five Talents] our Two [Talen]ts, or even our O[ne...]—awful responsibility!—methinks we may well [...] are there few that be saved?"—and again, "who may [...] the day of his coming? and who may stand when he appeareth." [...] These are solemn, and awful enquiries to us who every day [...] so far short of our duties,—but thanks be to the Lord who [...] given us the victory, there is plenteous Redemption in the [...] giving blood of the Lamb." though we have no righteousness of our own to cover us, yet may we come adorn'd in the snow white robes of Jesus Christ, our Lord, and with palms of victory in our hands.—oh let us praise him, let us adore him "who rideth above the heavens."—"Blessing, and honor and glory, and power, be unto him [t]hat sitteth upon the throne, and unto the Lamb, for ever, and ever." Oh, for the joyful sound of "Well done, good and faithful servant! "—[...] again,—"Come ye blessed of my father, inherit the kingdom prepared [for] you from the foundation of the world."—then may we cast our "crowns" [before] the throne" and sing Hosannas forever, and forever!

[October] 9

Have just return'd from the Sabbath School.—sometimes [...] hopes that the dear little lambs entrusted to us, are making [...] and that the Lord will see fit to bless our labours, [...] times, a cloud hangs over my mind as it relates [...] for our children appear to be too thoughtless to the [...] their everlasting peace.— May our heavenly [...] labourers, and myself, and it consistant [...] to see some fruits of our labours!—yea, [...]gents, and bless his cause!—[...]ings reach [...] what {....}[63]

---

[63] Regrettably, the journal is particularly fragmented through this section.

Sabbath Day

Spent in Religious Exercises as usual.—Prayer, reading the word of God,—attending on the School, and visiting the Sick.—Took a sweet walk with a Female friend, the weather delightful.—Oh how delightful to view the varied scenery around. and the beauties which the lavish hand of a kind Parent scatters on every hand.—It is for those to enjoy it who:

"With a propriety that none can feel,
But who, with filial confidence inspired,
Can lift to heaven on unpresumptuous eye,
And smiling say—'My Father made them all.'"—

No Preaching in the Village to day.

October 29

Heard a most appropriate Sermon from Mr. McGuire yesterday.—it was a Burial sermon, and well adapted to the occasion.—his Text was from the 1st Epistle of St. John, the 2nd Chapter, and 17th Verse. "The world passeth away" etc.—it was a striking lesson to the living! and I pray that all present, both Saint, and Sinner, may have received the solemn warning to their everlasting profit.— may *I* have received to edification and spiritual improvement, the Evangelical truths breathed from the lips of a faithful ambassador of our heavenly Master, on this last Sabbath day!—oh, it was sweet to respond in the divine liturgy of our Church to this holy Man of God!—after the service of the Church, and the sermon was concluded, the burial service was solemnly perform'd over *two graves* by the Rev. Mr. McGuire.—how awful, how solemn the warning!

November 1

Have just return'd from visiting some sick friends on the other side of the Rappahannock.—Am disappointed that the Rev. Mr. Wydown has not fulfill'd his appointment in this place.—but I suppose the dampness of the weather has prevented him.

November 11

Have spent this morning of the Lord's own holy day, in Prayer, and in the reading of the word of God, and in teaching two poor Children their lessons from the holy Book, these two Girls have promised to come to me for instruction on the morning of every Sabbath day.—may the divine Master who I endeavour to serve, enable me to give them by his holy Spirit that religious improvement which may be to their benefit, and his glory!—Heavenly Parent,

bless my labours!—I feel this morning much engaged, and very happy—I have
for a few days had darken'd seasons, but it has pleased him whom my soul
loveth, to dissipate them, and to bid darkness flee, the sun-beams of his
righteousness, have again burst on me with redoubled splendour.—oh, how can
I enough glorify the God of my salvation!—oh that my besetting sin might never
again assail me!—that the thoughts of my heart might again never wander from
him whom my soul loveth!—oh my God let me each day live closer, and more
close to thee! and give me, oh give me that entire holiness of heart for which I
pant!

Yesterday we had a short, but very interesting Sermon from a spiritual
young Brother of the Methodist Church, he afterwards perform'd the burial
service over the Grave of a Lady recently dead. His manner was solemn and
impressive,—he did me the favor to spend the evening with me in my own
house, I prevail'd on some of my young female friends to join us, and we had a
sweet evening, spent very much to the satisfaction of us all, the youthful Davis,
while discoursing to us on spiritual things appear'd in my [eye] like some
ministering Angel, sent for a few moments, to bless with his presence my
habitation.—sweet was the prayer he breathed ere he departed, oh that every part
of it may be answer'd!

Thursday Morn

Clouds and darkness have for some days shadow'd my mind.—an
unaccountable lowness of spirits!—why should I be sad if I live close to God?—
oh my divine Creator!—my heavenly Father! If I may presume to claim thee for
my Father,—but I too much fear that I am sometimes far from thee!—why
should my thoughts ever rest on ought but thee?—forgive, oh forgive my
besetting sin,—forgive the wandering thought of my heart, and take back thy
repentant child!

Saturday

God is good!—The clouds have dispersed, and my mind again illumin'd
by the effulgent beams diffused by the presence of that great, and merciful One
who can at one irradiate the gloom, and dispel every shade,—I have loved
sometimes on a Summer's day, to watch the clouds as they break, and disperse
themselves, and flee away before the bright beams of the Sun, when bursting
forth in all its splendour, it dissolves by its vivifying warmth the humid vapours
which had for a while overshadow'd it. and gilding by its darting rays the
ethereal blue of a mid-day sky. I have loved to mark the Clouds thus dispersing,

thus dissolving, thus melting all, and vanishing away, leaving the sky more
sweetly serene, more bright, more pure, than it had even been before.—Thus it
is methinks with the Christian's mind.—though there may be seasons observed
by flitting Clouds, yet so soon as the Sun of righteousness shall arise, the God of
our Salvation irradiate us with his presence, biding darkness flee.—oh then how
soon is every doubt, and fear, and misty care dispel'd!—all then is sunshine in
the peaceful bosom.—we feel than that the ever blessed Jesus is our portion, that
we are the Creation of his power, every moment depending on his bounties, and
that without continual renewals of his grace we are nothing.—and oh what a
happiness to confide in him!—to know that {....} we are dependant on one who
is true, and just, and merciful in all his dealings, who rules all things for the
best,—to *know* and to *feel*, that this state of dependance on him, frees us from
the tyranny of Satan, and the Slavery of an unjust world.—for,- "He is the
freeman whom the truth makes free, and all are Slaves beside."—it is while
enjoying feelings such as these, that we are fill'd with a peace of mind which
passeth all understanding and which the world with all its glittering allurements
can neither give nor take away,—Happy are we when we can thus look to the
Author, and finisher of our faith, and like Job of old, exclaim—"For I know that
my redeemer liveth, and that he shall stand at the latter day."—happy are we,
when thus fill'd with a holy resignation, thus gently led, we held ourselves up to
him, who groan'd, and bled, and died, that we might live.—Oh, my Saviour
keep me thus forever, and let me roam no more!—how I love to dwell on these
happy seasons, when faith is strong, and every doubt dispel'd.—when all is
sunshine, when I forget the clouds that have sometimes intervened, and as they
flited over, obscured for a while the lovely Landskape, *without effacing it.*—Oh
when shall my panting trembling spirit wing its way to that divine abode where
clouds and darkness are no more,—where everlasting day excludes the night,—
where peace forever reigns!—and may I hope to gain admission there?—may I
hope that this restless, throbing tenant of my bosom, this weak, imperfect,
sensate heart, out of which "are the [...] of Life."—oh may I hope that it may be
at last completely sanctified to thee oh, Lord!—perfect it in holiness my
heavenly Father! for without holiness none shall be admitted to thy presence.—
enable me to "keep my heart with all diligence" so may every thought of it be
dedicated to the.—keep me, oh keep me King of kings, and let me roam no
more.—So may I at the last be admitted to the presence of God the Father, God
the Son, and God the holy Ghost, the coeternal three, and live and dwell forever
there!—live to all eternity in that heavenly place of rest where Sin, and sorrow
cannot enter, but where an innumerable host, a multitude not to be number'd,

"of all nations, and kindreds, and people, and tongues, shall stand before the throne, and before the Lamb, cloth'd with white robes, with palms in their hands." Singing glory for ever to him who hath wash'd, and redeem'd them with his blood.—amidst this holy band will be seen the blessed souls of them that were slain for the word of God, and for the testimony which they bore."— sainted Martyrs! how bright will be your crowns of glory!—and there too, in that holy band of the just made perfect, will be seen, lovely among ten thousand, the faithful Ministers of God, they who here on earth have endeavour'd to propagate his name, who have labour'd in his cause.—they who for his name's sake, have endured deprivations, and persecutions, and distress,—yes, amidst ten thousand, they will appear lovely, all array'd in "the beauty of holiness," in the spotless robes of a Saviour's righteousness—even now in my "Mind's eye" methinks I behold them, presenting themselves, and their flock to Jesus—their *flock*, saved through their instrumentality!—*themselves*, and their *flock*, saved by the *blood* of the *Lamb*—methinks too I hear, or seem to hear, the joyful salutation of "Well done thou good and faithful Servant!"—and again,—"Enter thou into the joy of thy Lord!"—and still again in Fancy's ear I seem to hear, the gracious welcome, of,—"Come ye blessed of my Father, inherit the crown laid up for you from the foundation of the World!"—Yes, holy Men of God, great will be your reward in heaven!—and oh, that I may be permited to greet you there, I who here on earth so much love and reverence you,—for sweet, yea, very sweet to me are the peaceful messages you bring!—and there is one among you, whom here on earth I shall never see again, one who is perhaps destin'd to receive a Martyr's crown, *one persecuted holy Man of God.*—with him I have delighted to share sweet counsel and to talk of all the lovely things preach'd by him in God's own sanctuary.—oh, when I have been thus conversing with him of things sacred, and divine, and beheld his countenance irradiated by the inspiring truths he utter'd I could almost imagine that I beheld the brilliant halo which Painters use to designate their Saints, suspended o'er his lovely brow,— so bright to me was the countenance of one, who came like an Angel of Light, bearing with him the messages, of Peace, and Love, and Joy!—but *him* I shall *never* behold *again on earth*, he labours in a far distant Land.—Persecuted Andrus! I hope to meet thee on a shore of better promise!—Peace be to thee my Missionary Friend!—and though thou dost.—"Forsake thy Father Land,
　　　　　Kindred, and friends, and pleasant home.
　　　　　O'er many a rude barbarian strand,
　　　　　In exile though thou roam,
　　　　　Walk there with God, and thou shalt find,

doublc for all thy faith resign'd."

Oh, I do so reverence, so love, and admire the faithful Ministers of God, that I would have all Men like them!—but alas all Men will not be pure and holy like them! and by ungodly Men they are persecuted, but they will be "ministering spirits," while the ungodly "lie howling."—Yes very lovely to me are the messengers of Peace, and Joy and Love.—they who bring glad tidings of great Joy!

How beauteous are their feet,
who stand on Zion's hill,
and bring Salvation on their tongues,
And words of peace reveal.

And oh what a happiness must it be to them who are above the beggarly elements of this world, to think that they have *souls* for their hire!—souls saved through *their instrumentality*!—surely it is a glorious calling!—I am perhaps what the World may deem an enthusiast, but I shrink from the World, for it is too often selfish, and unfeeling and too often ready to throw the imputation of Enthusiasm, or romance on all such feelings as do not assimilate with its own.— but I trust in those regions which I love to contemplate, in that heaven to which I lift my hopes, that there are some better modifications for these things.—and oh, methinks I would not for all the treasures of this world, relinquish these, the lovely visions of my mind! and which I hope will one day be realized in heaven.—it is *there the treasure* is.—Yes, "verily there is a reward laid up for the righteous, doubtless there is a God who judgeth the earth"—Then let me press on, and may god of his infinite mercy enable me to gain the reward,—*the Treasure that is in Heaven!*

Thursday Eve

Have received a long and very spiritual Letter from my Episcopal friend, my Brother in Gospel bonds, Thomas Smith,—it is sweet to be thus remember'd when distance separates us from those we esteem, and it is particularly gratifying thus to commune by Letter with one who has early enlisted under the banners of Christ, and who is now perhaps more than two hundred miles distant,—but neither time, nor space, can controul the minds that are in Christ Jesus,—his Spirit guides, and actuates his people,—his Spirit prompts the sweet remembrance,—and writes in the bonds of Christian fellowship his faithful followers.

Tuesday Morn

Return'd yesterday from Mr. Turner's, where I had been for a few days, the Rev. Mr. Belknap return'd with me and spent the day.—he looks methinks as if he would not long be a sojourner here, his declining health appears to be hurrying him rapidly to the end of his earthly pilgrimage.—he spent a friendly, and social day with me, the last perhaps that it shall ever spend with this Man of God, for this day he starts in search of a milder Clime.—methinks I shall never forget this, his last visit to me,—he staid until after Candle light, and just before he departed, bent before the Throne of Grace, with myself, and my old domestic, and breathed an affecting prayer.—he pray'd that should he never more see me on earth, we might yet meet again in heaven, and when he had ended, and rose up, and stood before me, holding out his hand to say farewell,—oh, methought at that moment, I could almost have immagined him already a beatified being,— so pale, so spiritual was his appearance!—Fare thee well, my Presbyterian friend! my brother in Christ!—may thy prayer be answer'd! and if we meet no more on earth, oh may we yet meet again in those blissful abodes, where Christian friends all shall meet, and dwell forever together in the presence of God forever!

Tuesday Eve

Have been much indisposed all day with a severe Cold, and almost insupportable pressure on my Lungs.—how weak, how fragile, are these tabernacles of Clay!—a trifling accident, or even a humid atmosphere, can in a moment disorder the whole machinery.—surely it ought only to be prized as being loan'd us for a while, by our divine Creator, as a tenement for that nobler part, the immortal Soul!—Yet a little while, and this Soul, "immortal as its sire" will be call'd away,—yet a little while, and I may be,—a Sainted Maid in heaven!

December 8

The Friend of God,—the Friend of Man, is no more,—he whom my thoughts delighted to rest upon, has got home to his Father's house before me,— the benign[...], the gentle spirit of Andrus, has sought the bosom of its Father, and its God,—beyond the reach of persecution now, he makes one, lovely amidst ten thousand of that shining host, that holy band of the just made perfect, o'er his lovely brow is suspended a sparkling Crown of glory while he joins the innumerable throng singing around the Throne the praises of redeeming love.— he has got home a little before me, and even now he waits me on a Shore of better promise,—yet a little while and he will welcome me there,—even now methinks I Hear the joyful shout of,—"Come ye blessed of my Father."—and oh, will it be permited to my favorite Minister?—to Andrus, in whom my soul delighted,—will it be permited to him to present me to the blessed Jesus?—will Andrus present me as one of the seals to his Ministry?—as one of the ransomed of his flock?—ransomed by the blood of the Lamb!—ransomed through the instrumentality of my favorite Minister!—oh, let me dwell on this thought!—let me believe that it may be—that it *will* be,—surely it cannot be a chimera of a mind deeply affected with the subject!—it is a sweet idea!—I delight to dwell on the lovely vision, for I hope one day, to find it not an untrue one.—Yes, I love to anticipate the time, when I shall meet Andrus in Heaven!—meet him in the presence of God the Father,—God the son, and God the Holy Ghost,—the co-eternal three!—no longer the *persecuted* Andrus!—no longer then "the Man of sorrows, and acquainted with grief."—but the *happy* Andrus! basking in the sun-shine of his Father's home, safely shelter'd from every storm!—for Persecution cannot enter there; and Hatred, and Envy, and Malice, with all the invenom'd, and Fiend-like train, will {....}[64] flee that blissful Port, where nought but happy spirits dwell—oh, that I may gain admittance there!—oh that I may meet Andrus in Heaven!—meet him "in Christ to part no more"!—"oh happy day, when Christians meet, to part no more!"—And yet how my heart bleeds, when I think of all he might have suffer'd ere yet his gentle and benignant spirit, took its upward flight,—perhaps his Fever being a contagious one, he might not have had even one kind hand to wipe from his lovely brown, the cold, damp dews of Death, to impress on it the affectionate kiss, and drop on it the sympathetic tear,—Like his divine Master, all might have fled him!—perhaps he was forsaken of all.—left in the last agony,—left to combat all alone, with his last trying enemy,—perhaps in that dred moment, he too might have cried,— "Abba, Father, all things are possible unto thee, take away this cup from me, nevertheless not what I will, but what thou wilt." -- Oh I shall weep afresh, when I hear the whole sad Tale of all he suffer'd— But have I said that in the last dread agony he might have bene left all alone?—ah, surely no, for if every earthly friend forsook him, his Heavenly Father still was near,—then in that last awful struggle of expiring mortality, then, even then, was the exceeding great,

---

[64]At this point the original version of the document is not in the correct chronological order and I have determined what appears to be the most likely possibility based on context. Several pages are placed here before the next entry, whereas in the original they stand alone, undated.

and very precious promise realized,—" I will never leave thee, or forsake thee."—Oh, Christian! thou hast found "the arms of Jesus, as soft as downy pillows are."—My departed Christian Friend! I shall often think of thee,—think of all thy wondrous worth—"Beloved 'til Life can charm no more, and mourn'd 'til pity's self is dead,"—but with the help of God, thou wilt be sweetly, and not bitterly mourn'd, for Christians cannot mourn as tho' they were without hope,— with a sadly pleased remembrance then, let me think of Andrus.—and God enable me to press on, looking in faith to the blessed promises of a Crucified Saviour,—so may I hope ere a little time has fled, to be admitted to the glorious presence of the God-head, to live, and dwell forever there.—and there too may I meet again my favorite Andrus,—meet him where sin and sorrow are no more, where every tear is dried, and where the Wicked cease from troubling, where the weary are at rest."—for "There remaineth a rest for the People of God."—

Methinks even now I behold the lovely, and serious countenance of my Friend, when not long before his departure from America, he in one of his delightful conversations with me, recited to me some beautiful passages from Henry Kirk White's Poems,—that day there was a slight shade of melancholy hung over him, the expression of his countenance I never can forget, he exclaim'd in that beautiful stanza from White,

"But hush, my fond heart, hush,
There is a shore of better promise,
And I hope at last we two shall meet
In Christ to part no more."

Oh yes,! yet a little while, and I trust and hope "we two shall meet in Christ to part no more."—the Friend of God, the friend of Man is no more! "his bones have taken possession of the promised land, and rest in the glorious hope of the final and universal triumph—Jesus over the God's of this world."— Andrus has closed his eyes forever on the things of time and sense.—now far beyond the reach of *Persecution*, he wakes to raptures in a world of Love and Joy. perhaps at this very moment, from his elevated height of happiness, it is permitted him to behold some of his Christian friends, who are still pilgrims, and strangers in this val of tears.—perhaps now, even in this very moment, it is permitted him to behold the inmost recesses of the heart of *one devoted American Friend, one native of Virginia*, who would have *died* to have served him—oh, I have remember'd him in my every prayer!—but he needs not now my feeble petitions.—let me pray for myself, for the *poor imperfect J.L.* has need of prayer—then let me pray without ceasing! for temptations, and trials even now beset me, but I look to a crucified Redeemer, and trust that his Grace will be all sufficient for me"—oh that my walk may be closer, and more close to God! so that at the last I may come to his eternal joy.—the Christian's Anchor is sure, and steadfast.—Andrus, I hope to meet [...] a shore of better promise." where Friendship becomes double refined, and worth is crown'd by Sainted Love.—oh, let me press on,—I have Heaven in view!

December 22

Have just return'd from the house of mourning, from the Chamber of Death!—pale lifeless lump of Mortality! solemn the warning, that seem'd to arise from that cold and motionless form!—I beheld consign'd to its kindred dust, all that now remains of her who once was lovely, once was gay, animated, and brilliant!—she who once sparkled in the gay assembly, and by her beauty, and wit, fascinated her admiring beholders,—alas all has fled!—what is she now?—oh thoughtless mortals!—ye who are now preparing your costly ornaments to deck your perishable bodys, for the brilliant, and gay assembly on Thursday night. oh behold that narrow dwelling, and learn humility!—there lies inter'd the remains of one who once was lovely, and admired like yourselves.— behold, and meditate! let that *uncover'd* Grave remind you, that you too must die.—behold oh thoughtless Beauty! and oh turn, ere yet it be too late!—that fleeting moments are too precious to be danced away in giddy mirth,—return ye, return!

December 25

The Nativity of a Saviour!—This day a God deign'd to descend to earth, deign'd to be clothed in suffering mortality, and to experience, (sin alone excepted) all the evils incident to human nature,—Let Christians hail with triumph this auspicious day, for this day a babe was born!—a Saviour came to make atonement of a guilty world, he came the herald of Love, and peace, and joy!—Oh, he came the bearer of mercy to the fallen Children of Adam!—for he came to bind up the broken heart—to set the captive prisoners free; he himself the precious ransom!—oh glorious day, that usher'd in a Saviour! which brought "good tidings of great joy."—"good tidings of great joy" that shall reach from pole to pole, til Earth's remotes bound shall hear the joyful sound, Until every Nation of every tongue, of every tribe, and of every people shall understand, and know, that God is Lord, and that for *us*, for *them*, was this day born a Saviour, "which is Christ the Lord."—And oh may the time speedily arrive, when all shall be fill'd with the knowledge of God, when every knee shall be fill'd with the knowledge of God, when every knee shall bow to the sceptre of Jesus, and

when righteousness shall cover the earth, as the seas cover the great deep!—
speed, oh, speed, the time my heavenly Father!—Yes, on the 25th day of this
month a Saviour descended to earth, the came to suffer, the just for the unjust—
"was ever love like this."—for us he bled, for us he died!—oh Christian think
how vast the debt!—remember the agony in the Garden of Gethsemene.—turn
thine eye to the brow of Calvary,—visit in thought the Sepulcre of Jesus, the
place where thy Lord was laid, thy crucified, but now risen Redeemer.—think of
these things Christian, ponder in thy heart, God's redeeming love, and think how
vast the debt! how great the sacrifice!—then oh Christian say,—can'st thou ever
love enough, can'st thou ever serve enough!—oh remember a God came down
to earth to bleed and die for thee, for thou hast been bought with a price, even
with the blood of Jesus—who is now, even now interceding at God's right hand
for thee.—Christian thy sins are done away! Jesus hath bloted them from the
book of remembrance, and in their stead, he hath placed thy name in the Lamb's
fair book of Life.—Jesus is thy friend!—and oh remember that he bore the
heavy Cross, the brutal jests, the buffetings of a licentious Mob,—he bore them
all for thee!—that thou might live!—and wilt thou not then in thy turn, bear the
cross for such a precious friend!—oh surely yes!—and let each Christian then
exclaim,—Come persecutions, or distress, or pain, or want, or death, I will bear
them all for Jesus's sake, for him who first loved me!—He sought me when I
was a stranger, when I was wandering in the mazes of sin, when I was the child
of error and at enmity with him.—yea, he drew me with the Cords of his
heavenly love, he purified my will, so that I could no longer strive against his
power, his goodness, and his wondrous love.—then it was that I could exclaim,
here Lord, take me for I am thine, " I give myself to thee 'tis all that I can do"—
I surrender up the arms of my rebellion, "against thee only have I sin'd" and yet
thou had'st had mercy on me ere yet it was too late.—Jesus my all!—oh how
can I enough magnify, and adore thee, thou precious Lamb! and oh if I have
found favor in thy sight, exemplify it Lord, by making me an instrument in thy
Service, let me be devoted to thy cause.—for it was thou who pardon'd my sins
and bid the Captive live.—it was thy spirit that breathed on me, and whisper'd to
my troubled soul, "Thy sins are forgiven"—thy spirit bid me "go in peace."—
And oh my Saviour thou hast indeed given me, that peace which passeth all
understanding, and which [...] World can neither give, nor take away.

December 27

Oh how I grieve for some of the thoughtless inhabitants of this Village—
even now they are preparing for the gay assembly, the dance, the festive

party!⁶⁵—this night will the thoughtless beauty deck herself in gay apparel, but could she have permitted herself on Saturday last to have visited the Chamber of Death, and there beheld, the remains of her who once was lovely, one too was gay,—had she beheld the once admired, but now lifeless form consign'd to its last narrow dwelling.—she surely would have learnt a lesson of humility!—Oh, thoughtless fair one! who art now, even now, arraying thyself for the splendid ball, go pause over yonder uncover'd Grave! meditate for a little while, then come again to that same spot, on the twelfth day of this month, and hear from the burial service the solemn words,—"I am the resurrection and the life."—hearken again and hear, "Dirt to dirt, ash's to ash's."—then listen yet once again, and thou wilt hear the clay cold sod, as it falls heavy on the last narrow bed of a Sister worm.—say thoughtless Beauty! shall not these things alarm thy sleeping conscience, and humble thee!—return ye, return!

This day recalls to my mind some affecting remembrances,—it was on the morning of St. John's day, exactly two years since, that I cross'd the Rappahannock with some kindred spirits, *they were Christians! Andrus*, the now beatified Andrus! was then a sojourner with us, he made one of our happy little party,—the weather was uncommonly fine and we all united our Voices in singing sweet hymns of praise to the Deity, as the Boat glided rapidly over.—never shall I forget the inimitable Sermon, preach'd by our friend Andrus that day in the Church of Port Royal, and address'd to his Masonic Brethren, he chose the subject of the good Samaritan,—"Go thou and do likewise." was his Text.—but now, "Joseph restes from his labours, and his works do follow him."

The twelfth day of this month will be to me a solemn season, on that day I hope to received the Sacrament of the Lord's Supper form the Rev. Mr. McGuire, it has been long since I had an opportunity of commemorating the love of a crucified and risen Redeemer,—crucified for my sins, and risen for my justification.—oh let me in the intermediate time examine my heart! let me more than ever remember the debt of love I owe, and the glorious plan of Salvation which opens the Gates of heaven to all true believers,—a Saviour, a bleeding Saviour, has open'd the way, and invited *all* to *come* who *will*.—methinks this ordinance on the twelfth, will be to me peculiarly affecting, when last I shared this feast of love in my own Church, I received the consecrated elements from a

---

⁶⁵ The "festive party" here refers to the Feast of Saint John the Evangelist, celebrated on December 27 in Western Christendom. At this historical juncture, even in what was apparently becoming a much less rigid, formal liturgical religious culture, feast days of certain prominent saints were still observed. These general societal references provide valuable insight into the entire religious ethos of the time period.

hand that is now mouldering in silent dust,—it was my favorite *Andrus* who shared an distributed this holy pledge of his divine Master's love.—it was from his hand I received it, when I last received it in the Episcopal Church.—but he is gone! he has ascended to *his* Father, and *my* Father, and now he drinks the fruit of the vine new in his Father's kingdom,—yes, the hand which once presented the sacred symbols of a Saviour's love, now moulders in the silent grave,—but oh that soul, a lovely, and brilliant emination of the deity who gave it, shall live forever!—Often shall I remember with a sadly pleased remembrance, the worth of my departed friend, for even from the first of my acquaintance with him, I thought I perceived in him a kindling spark which would light him on to glory,—a spirit that would lead him from the common track of Life,—and it has been even so,—for methinks in some things he appear'd to have had the standard of his divine master full in view, and to have pursued his track.—but he is gone! and oh what a glorious death!—a Martyr to the Christian cause—a faithful servant to him he loved! even his Lord, and Master the blessed Jesus! whose commands he literally obey'd.—but he has his reward!—even now he doubtless wears a Martyr's brilliant crown,—how high must be his grade of happiness!—how elevated his seat in Heaven!—

—On the twelfth day of this month too another solemn Ordinance will draw my attention.—I shall witness the burial service perform'd over the Grave of a departed Sister, shall hear the cold sod, sound hollow, as it falls heavy over the last narrow dwelling of a lump of morality,—may my soul be profited by these things! and be more, and assimilated to a Saviour's image!—Death daily calls his millions at a meal—and have I said that on the twelfth, I shall witness these things!—presumptious me!—for ought I know my soul may ere that time be required.—how arrogant am I!—

"How many precious souls are fled
To the vast regions of the dead,
Since to this day the changing Sun
through his last yearly period run!"

How arrogant it is in us finite Beings to say that thus it *shall* be, or *will* be!—Ere the twelfth day of this month my soul may be summon'd to stand on account of the deeds done in the body.—awful idea—may I dare to ask myself how might stand the account!—I who always feel myself the least of all,—too weak of faith,—fragile and timid, ever fearing to do *wrong*, I seem to do *nothing*.—"for to will is always present with me, but how to perform that which is good, I find not, for the good that I would do, I do not, but the evil that I would not, that I do."—"Oh wretched me," might I will exclaim, was there not one stronger and mightier than I,—one that is omnipotent to save!—even he who shed his blood for me,—he who died that I might live!—leaning on his bosom, I will look to him, and put my sure trust in him, for it only through him my blessed Lord, and Master, that I can hope for justification.—clothed in the white robes of his imputed righteousness, I may hear undismay'd the awful summons, and even exult that the freed spirit should burst its imprisonment of clay.—oh, I trust I shall "be more than conqueror through him that loved me."— When I feel my shortcomings, it is yet a comfort to me to know that there is one who is the searcher of all hearts, he knows the desire of mine, he knows that tit pants after holiness and complete sanctification.—for I know that "without holiness none can see the Lord."—"be ye perfect, even as your Father which is in heaven is perfect" he knows that I pant for this, and a more perfect conformity to his image.—he knows my desire, and my groanings are not hid from him.—oh, I trust he will speed the time when I shall be completely sanctified to him!—when I shall be ripe for glory, and worthy of being admited into his heavenly kingdom, there to dwell in his presence forever,—to live forever around his Throne, with his host of glorified spirits, singing with them the praises of redeeming love,—there may I again join in singing sweet hymns of praise with some dear Christian who hath got home before me to his Father's house,—Andrus perhaps with thee, I may raise again the hymn of praise!—how sweet will be the anthems re-echo'd by the vault of Heaven!—and what a glorious company will be found in that blessed place where Jesus reigns!—oh how I love to contemplate with an eye of Faith that heaven to which my Soul aspires!—and to hope that the day will speedily arrive when I may hear the joyful salutation of,—Soul thou hast done thy best, thy strivings whilst thou wert yet on earth, were not in vain,—Thy Lord and Master beheld the desire of thy heart, he witness'd too with pitying eye the warfare between the spirit and the flesh.—thou hast been sprinkled with the precious blood of his rich-attonement—soul thou hast done thy best,—enter thou into the joy of thy Lord!—Oh, how my waking, meditations, and even my sleeping visions, delight to dwell on these things!—I will hope one, and I will look with an eye of faith, to that blessed reward laid up in reversion for those who love the Lord.—what tho I gain but the lowest seat, even that will satisfy my humble spirit—one little corner, so it be in *Heaven*, will be enough!—oh if I can only be where Jesus is, and associate with his holy band, and dwell forever in his presence, and sing forever around his Throne, it will be happiness for me!—I sometimes think that there are different grades of happiness in heaven.—that for *such as me*, the lowest seat is quite enough, for oh, *I* of *myself merit nothing*!—it is my blessed

Jesus,—it is only through him, I can hope for even one little corner!—well, I may hope to behold his face, to mingle with his Saints, and to meet again my favorite Andrus!—let me press on, my Saviour aids me, he reach's out his arm, that I may climb to heaven!

• 1822 •

January 7

Have received a Letter from my valued brother in the Lord, Thomas Smith, if the Lord spares us, he will be with me on the twelfth, and he says, he expects to be accompanied by a Minister of our Church,—God is good, he deals graciously with me!

January 12

My Heavenly Father has spared me to behold this day, and may he make it a day of profit to me!—this day may I receive the sacred symbols of his love, to the refreshment of my soul!

January 13

Have again been permitted to approach my heavenly Father's board,— and received I hope to the profit of my soul, the hallow'd symbols of his love, have received them from a Minister of my own Church,—oh, I have yet once again been permitted to taste of the consecrated elements! to eat, and drink, in remembrance that Christ died for me!—glorious privilege may it be so sanctified to me, that I may at the last be admitted to the marriage supper of the Lamb, may be found one amongst the number of wise virgins, and with them drink the fruit of the vine new in our Father's kingdom!—Yesterday was a day of much refreshment to my soul, a day too in which my feelings were to be touch'd, and much excited.—We had an excellent, and appropriate sermon from the Rev. McGuire, and when that twas finish'd and he had administer'd the Sacrament of the Lord's Supper, we then proceeded to the Grave of our departed Sister, there to attend to the solemn burial service of our Church, there to witness the last awful and impressive duty perform'd over the Dead.—oh that it may be more, and more impress'd by these things, that I may ponder them in my heart, and be profited by them!

—Yesterday too, I had the satisfaction of entertaining in my own house, some friends very dear to me.—Brother Smith after joining us at the sacramental table, return'd home with me, and in addition to him, I had four of my Village friends whom I highly value,—namely, Frances, and Caroline, Mary and Louisa.—and in the Evening we had an encrase to our little circle, the Rev. Mr. Davis, of the Methodist Church, with one, or two, other *seriously disposed* sisters.—Oh, I find it very sweet to associate with the people of God, and those who love God, and his people!—Brother Smith has promised to come again soon, and bring with him the Rev. Mr. Clapham, the Minister whom he had expected to accompany him on the Twelfth to the Village.—May God speed their coming! —Yesterday was to me a day of much interest,—in the morning I felt myself deeply affected, and my mind was perhaps somewhat agitated before I left my own house to attend divine worship, I wish'd for some kind, spiritual friend to have unbosom'd all my feelings to, but there was none near, it was then I mentally exlaim'd,—what tho all creature comforts fail? tho' I converse with me, and to assist me in examining my heart?—shall I for one moment despair?—ah, no! there is one supreme over all, one who knows better than any earthly friend the secret windings of my heart.—and he will better teach me how to examine it.—I said *I will look to God alone*!—it was in that blessed moment, I felt *a return* to that will of my heavenly Father, which brought me low at the foot of the Cross, there to wait, til all his will be done.—it was in this frame of mind that I dared to approach his hallow'd board.—And oh, it was good for me to go!—for in that moment I felt that I could look to Jesus and be happy. I now feel that *he is my all*, and as if nought on earth could shake the happy serenity of my soul,—Surely it is good to be refresh'd at our Father's board, to renew with him our covenanted vows, and [plight] our faith anew! of we derive from thence a bliss, and peace in believing, which the untied powers of Satan, and the World are unable to shake.—Surely I am at this moment in the happiest frame of mind!—sweetly yielding myself up to him who hath wash'd, and redeem'd me wit his own precious blood, I seem to feel that my heart can know no other inmates save "Faith, Hope, and Charity."—oh, may it be ever thus!—and "Faith, Hope, and Charity." be forever my Motto!

January 24

Have just parted with some dear Christian friends who have been staying several days with me,—it is good for Christians to meet together, and hold sweet converse of the blessedness of those, who have God for their portion,—to talk of the things that belong unto God.

Have been attending a Masonic Burial, the Rev. Mr. McGuire, performing the Service.—William Bernard lately deceased, has been buried with *Masonic honors*, there were some of us Ladies, who paid what respect we could, by following the procession of Masons,—the whole had a solemn, and pompous appearance,—the Body was posited in the family Vault of the deceased, near his House on the opposite side of the Rappahannock.—it was borne across the River in a large flat Boat, in which the Masons also went—we Ladies, and a few Gentlemen who were not Masons, follow'd the large Boat, in a little skiff, which

had belong'd to the deceased.—The Rev. Mr. McGuire, merely perform'd the
burial Service at the Vault, and exhorted a little.—there was an Eulogium
spoken by one of the Masonic Brethren, *in some parts not very appropriate.*—
And after all, what avail'd this wondrous show of Pomp?—could it have
recall'd the departed Soul, or given it a passport to the bless'd abodes,—oh, then
it had been well!—but alas the scene was closed!—it was finish'd!—for there is
not work beyond the Grave,—then what, what avail'd it, to the soul now gone
forever?—Oh! while I follow'd in the procession with other Ladies, in the rear
of the Masons, I thought of these things,—I thought too of one whose lowly
Grave was made in the wilds of Africa, *he too was a Mason* but no emblems of
his Order,—no pompous procession announced his worth to an assembled
Multitude.—no family burying ground,—no wall'd up Vault, received the cold
remains of the holy Many of God, but most probably, a little scraped up earth,
soded by some kind hand, now only marks to the passing traveler, the spot
where silently reposes the Bones of the Christian Hero,—oh, how very much
contrasted were the Characters of these two brother Masons!—the *one*, a Man of
pleasure, and of the World.—the *other* not of this world, but truly, *a Man of
God*,—and how very different most probably their burial—Over the Errors of
B[...]d,[66] let Charity draw her Vail, for he yet had some Virtues—virtues which
endear'd him to his friends, and the social circle.—but B[...]d, was *not* a Man of
God, his portion was of *this* world!—But oh *Andrus*! my dear Missionary
friend, it was given to *thee*, to look to a *better* kingdom, and thou hast won a
crown of more glory, than ever graced on earth a Monarch's head!—thou wast
very lovely in Life!—thy Death was most glorious!—and honor's be thy
Grave!—on that consecrated spot may the green grass wave lovely,—and as the
Traveler treads softly by; may he behold the evening Sun shine sweetly on it.—
Even now, methinks I behold the rank Grass grow there, and wave as the breeze
pass's over it.—Yea, my departed Christian friend! thou wast indeed very lovely
in thy life, for thine was the beauty of Holiness—thou hast pass'd away thou
holy one; on earth thou wilt be seen no more,—the benevolent glance of thy
speaking eye shall no more beam on the benighted African, he shall listen in
vain for the soft sound of thy Voice, but thou wilt live in his remembrance, and
each succeeding generation will revere the name of Andrus, of him who guided
by the holy spirit of God, went like an angel of light, to irradiate a darken'd
Land, to plant there the standard of the Redeemer's Cross, and shed the beams

---

[66] Interestingly, she occasionally leaves the names of certain individuals out of her
text deliberately, which is the case here. The word is not missing from the text, as is the usual
circumstance when this symbol is used, rather she has chosen not to record it.

of light, and love, caught from the eminations of the Deity. he went to make the Desert bloom,—to proclaim to untutor'd Africans, the glad tidings of Salvation through the ever blessed name of Immanuel.—but he doubtless became ripe for glory, too pure for Earth! and his etherialized soul attracted to its long sought home, has mounted on a ray of glory to the [...] of its God.—the Sainted Martyr is doubtless now receiving his reward for the testimony which he bore for his divine Master whilst he labour'd here on earth in his sacred cause!—*Andrus*, thou art gone!—thou hast past away in thy glory, in the very prime of thy days, with all thine honors thick upon thee!—yes, thou hast past away from earth, like some lovely, fragrant flower, which tho gone, yet leaves it rich perfume behind,—for thou hast left behind thee a bright example for others to follow, and a spotless fame for thy friends to glory in.—*Africa*, to latest periods will remember that an *Andrus lived*, will remember that Philanthropic one, who left his Father, Mother, Friends and native land, that he might burst the fetters of superstition, and reach to Africa's sons, so Africa's sons might yet be free.— teach them how they might escape from the bondage of error, and find freedom in the unsearchable rich's of Christ,—find it in the everlasting liberty of the gospel—Lovely Beam! thou hast past away, and left a brilliant track behind.— the lustre of thy bloom will be remember'd, for the perfume of it remains.—and oh, thy spring has revived on a fairer world than this, even a Spring that shall last to all eternity!—a bloom immortal [...] heavens!—Then hallow'd be that lowly Bed, in the wilds of Africa, where thy clay cold relics lie!—there may the Evangelized Heathen pause, and w in the evening's sun shall gild with its parting rays, the rank grass's that waves over it there as he pauses, may he drop the tear of sadly pleased remembrance, while he points it out, to the passing traveler, and exclaims,—*behold the Grave of Andrus*![67]

February 20

Spent the whole of yesterday with a Bridal party.—Perhaps I have for the *last* time beheld *Louisa, Mary, Frances* and *Caroline,* altogether in their own House.—these four amiable females, (and all of them my particular friends) I have always liken'd to four lovely flowers growing together on one stem, for thy have always appear'd to be knit together in the bonds of sisterly love.—a beautiful harmony subsisting among them!—Well, one lovely flower has been selected from the rest, and pluck'd by one who now wears it on his heart, professing to love and admire it.—may it be ever cherish'd there!—Louisa, the

---

[67] An entire sermon preached by Andrus was reprinted posthumously in the *Theological Repertory*

blooming and admired Louisa, on Monday last, became the Bride of the Rev.
Mr. Bryce of the Baptist Church.—it has been destin[ed] that he should woo,
and win this inestimable treasure.—May they both be happy! loving, and
beloved!—each, aiding on the other, in their spiritual, as well temporal
labours.—and when after a life well spent in the cause of him who died that they
might live, may they then in that today, when terrestial scenes shall close on
them forever, be found among the faithful and enjoy in heaven that happiness
that shall endure throughout Eternity!

> Around the peerless Bride be shed,
> Unnumber'd joys that may not cease;
> And by Jehovah's spirit led,
> May all her paths, be paths of peace!

Wednesday Night

Have had the pleasure of entertaining the Bride, and Bride groom.—they
have just left me, after spending a social evening, which we closed as Christians
should do, in Prayer, all of us uniting.—they leave the village early tomorrow,
perhaps never again to see it, when they left me, they entreated me to see them
in the morning to take leave.

Thursday Morn

Agreeable to promise, I have been on my leave-taking visit.—perhaps I
have bid adieu to dear Louisa, never to see her again on this side Eternity.—she
has just left Port-royal with the chosen of her heart, the Rev. Mr. Bryce,—well,
should I never see them again, in this world, they will yet have my prayers.—
may they be happy in Time, and in Eternity!

Friday Eve

Have this morning heard an excellent Sermon from the Rev. Mr. Peyton,
of the Methodist Church, he took for his text one I have often wish'd to hear
preach'd from.—"Fear not little flock, for it is your Father's good pleasure to
give you the kingdom." He made a good discourse from it, and comforting to
Christians.

March 7

Have just return'd from hearing an excellent discourse from a favorite
Brother of the Methodist Church, the Rev. Mr. Davis.—Oh, that this Youthful
soldier who has early, and zealously, enlisted under the banners of Christ may

be the means of bringing many to the sacred standard of his heavenly Master!—May the Gospel spread, no matter under what name!—oh may it take the wings of the morn[68] [...]ing, and speed its way swiftly to the remotest corners of the ear[th] until *all* shall be *fulfill'd*!

Saturday Morn

Last night again, I seem'd to set like another Mary at the feet of Jesus, sweetly hearing the sacred and divine Truths as they were faithfuly deliver'd by his youthful embassador, the Rev. Mr. Davis,—the text was from the 3 Chapter of St. Paul's epistle to the Ephesians, 8, verse—"Unto me, who am less." etc.—That Grace to which he gave the praise appear'd in an eminent degree to rest on my Methodist Brother, whilst with the modesty of youth, and at the same time a liberty derived from him whose messenger he was he set forth the Truth as it was in Christ Jesus, and did justice to the subject of the inspired Apostle.—It was the very subject I wish'd to hear preach'd on.—alas, I always feel so little in my own eyes, that I for my part, may with much truth pronounce myself, *the very least of all*!

April 7

My little estray is welcome back, and I feel gratified that it has been sought for by one who though a young disciple in the Lord, I estimate highly, and I shall love my Note Book the more, as having excited the interest of my Christian friend to peruse its pages, may he (all unworthy as are my notes) have found some profit from the reading.—for the Christian who is always searching for good, will with the aid of his heavenly Master be sure to find it, even in the midst of what the *world* might deem rubbish.—the sweetest honey is sometimes extracted from the most insipid flowers!—God sometimes chooses to display his power by making the weakest instruments subservient to his purposes,—thus, Woman!—weak dependant Woman! is oftentimes elected to carry on his vast designs,—witness Apollos, mighty in learning and eloquence, and well skill'd in the scriptures, yet he great as he was, was yet taught the way of divine things more perfectly, by his two female friends Priscilla, and Aquilla.—and oh could I for one moment suppose that any one of my imperfect ideas, so faintly express'd in this my book of remembrance, could have kindled the spark for more brilliant ones in the mind of my dear young Brother (who is I think destin'd to be an ornament in the Church) I should [f]eel a joy which words cannot express, and I

---

[68]Order significantly reconstructed.

should think[69] myself well repaid for the short absence of this my Manuscript Volume.—Have been amusing myself with a peculiar kind of Talent with which my heavenly Father appears to have gifted me, cutting Paper in fanciful Devices; in one piece I have represented a kneeling Saint, and just above, is a Dove slightly sketch'd—the Motto—There is a way to way to Peace.—above the whole, is another, a Scriptural Motto, my favorite one, of "Faith, Hope, and Charity." and at the bottom of the piece, these lines of my own composition.

> Bending before the Throne of Grace,
> The Saint obtains a hallow'd ray;
> which beams a Saviour's steps to trace,
> And points through him the living way.

I have also executed another piece of this kind of work, to the Memory of one whose Virtue and Piety I love to remember,—he has departed from earth, to dwell forever in a brighter world,—In this little work I have represented a Tomb with an Urn on it, from it is ascending a spiritual and sainted form.—a Dove slightly sketch'd appears above, as if ready to receive, and welcome the Christian Martyr,—on the Tomb are Initials,—J,R,A.—in the centre of the Piece I have cut the word,—Glory and at the bottom of the piece are these lines composed by me for it,—

> The Warfare o'er,—The prize of glory won,
> Faithful he dies, and finds a rest above;
> And now O, Father! that they will is done,
> Thy *Andrus* meets thee perfect in Love.

Around the whole are these words,—A Tribute to Friendship, to Departed worth.—And O, it has been with a melancholy pleasure that I have thus traced with my Scissors, this memento of a Friend!—on it, the tear of *sensibility* has fallen, but I trust that *Religion* has sanctified the crystal tribute—

—Perhaps this way of spending time is not very profitable, but there are some who seem to think me a wonderful Artist, and that my work is altogether marvelous in their eyes—And yet it is not me, but I trust the grace of God which worketh in me, to will, and to do,—His breathing Spirit inspires me to devise, and execute,—at last it is *thus* I love to think, and to give him the Glory.—I believe we are never more happy than when we think that in all things, even the most trifling, we are {....}

---

[69]Order reconstructed, but even at this point in "mid-sentence" the flow of the text and content appears valid and fluid.

built on so sure a foundation [...]ng at the s[...] all that is praise-worthy, all that [is exce]llent, whe[...]acquir'd, to him the great giv[er of] every good, an[...] [...]s!—so may Genius, and all the rich acquirments of [...][...]d Learning, be sanctified to thy use oh, my God!—The Christian too, amongst other numberless recrea[...] [d]elights much in one that scarsely fails of breathing into [...F]ind a hallow'd peace.—delights to behold the hand of the Deity [...] the ever varying scenery of nature, "looking through nature, [u]p to Nature's God."—it is surely recreating in the highest [d]egree, to enjoy in the open air, the lovely prospects that present themselves to view, of hills, and dales, and fields, and murmur[ing] streams, and rivers rushing over their pebbled beds.—yes it is very refreshing, and of course (agreeable to my definition) very recreating, to both body, and mind, thus to ramble in the open air, (and whilst we ofttimes exhale the balmy breath of the den-scented flowers) to bless and praise the divine Author of all.— The great first cause! who thus scatters with an unsparing hand, blessings, an beauties around!—oh it is passing sweet when we can "lift to Heaven an unpresumptious eye, and smiling say, My Father made them all."—But words [w]ould fail to describe all the recreations of the Christian, whose very *avocations* yield a pe[...] which 'passeth all understanding," and which the world with all its glittering, and vain illusions, can neither given, nor take away.—"and tho[ugh] sometime a sigh may intervene, and down the cheek a tear of pity roll; a sigh, a tear so sweet, we wish not to controul."—Oh, it is sweet to be a Christian, and to bear a conscience [de]void of offence toward God, and Man!—To go on our way rejoicing in the Lord!—yea, I say again rejoice!—rejoice alway!—And now who may put in competition with the injoyments of the Christian, the assisting pleasures of a guilty world [...] The enjoyments of the Christian leave no sting behi[nd] [...] amidst trials, and the vicissitudes of Life, *still* the[...]

[...] is the anchor of those who have God for their [...]
for such "to smile at Fate, and wonder how th[...][...] for such to enjoy in the fullest extent of [...][...] and Friendship!
[...] [Amba]ssador of [...]—high, while engaged in the wors[hip][...] Trinity! [Oh how] sweet is the social worship pursue [...][...] [Lit]urgy of the Episcopal Church!—and now methinks[...] is not only social, but refreshing, or in other words, recreating]
[...] it is refreshing to the *Soul* and not laborious to the Bo[dy][Re]*reshment*, and *Recreation* appear to me *synonymous* terms.[...] now perhaps the Votary of the worldly pleasure may reply [...][...] this is too serious to apply to the terms in question.—w[...]

[ ]in should that even be admited, I will still go on to say that [bes]ides these, the delightful recreations of the Christian are unnumber'd—The Christian is quite an advocate for social visiting, and thinks it sweet for kindred minds to meet togeth[er] where "thought meets thought,"—and for them to talk together o[f] the gracious dealings of that God whom it is their desire to love supremely, and in loving him, they feel that they are bound to love one another,—very sweet is the bond of Christian friendship!—then surely it must be allow'd that the visiting of Christians is both social and Recreating.—and the more [so] as neither parade, or scandal are admited.—the Christian delights in acts of hospitality, and is particularly pleased when an opportunity occurs of entertaining the embassadors of God, those who come as heralds in his name, and bring salvation on their ton[gues]—the Christian feels this to be re[cre]ating, and social,—[...] that it is highly gratifying to gi[ve] even "a Cup of cold water in the name of a disciple" believi[ng] it shall meet with a disciple's reward.—for profitable to the soul is the society of [the is the society of] the Men of God!—The Scriptures shew forth in many places lovely examples of the social meetings of Christians.—Even the Saviour himself not unfrequently condescended to bless the social circle with his presence.—Ah, who may say how exquisitely sweet must have been the social parties at Bethany, when Jesus was entertain'd at the house of Martha and Mary, and [...]

Well though we cannot now behold Jesus in the [...] Martha, and Mary, and Lazarus.—yet he [...] our houses, be the bidden guest.—he may be spi-[...]s, and sweeten all our little social parties, [...] and take up his abode with us.—we may[...] him, whom "unseen we love."—Christian delights in [...]

September 7

Have been much pleased with the preaching of a Baptist Minister from Norfolk, his name Cornelious, and surely he is well named *Cornelious*! for he appears to be the *Centurian* of his *band*,—a bold Soldier in the cause of Christ—he holds back none of the truth, and is at the same time eloquent and persuasive—but perhaps it would have been better had he not have touch'd on the subject of Baptism; *there alone* I could *not* agree with him.—and yet if his opinions on that subject were supposed by him to be the only correct ones;— who shall condemn him? for he only utter'd what he perhaps thought it his duty to declare.—and tho I cannot agree with him on the subject of baptism, yet let me not blame him for endeavouring to enforce what he thinks right.—for every thing else beside that, I found it good to listen to him, for he spared neither [Saved] nor Sinner, and each, and every one of us, under the sound of his preaching, must have been reminded of, and felt our *short comings*!—I wish Cornelious may visit us again!

September 22

The Methodists preach to us often, and dearly do I love to hear them.— faithful and zealous; they appear to be indefatigable in the path of duty,— yesterday the youthful Davis, preach'd to us, and to day did me the favor to call on me, I always find much delight in conversing with him, he is truly inter[...] both in, and out of the Pulpit.—so young, and so devo[...] to the cause of his Lord, and Master!—methinks we might venture to say of him,—"behold an Israeli[...] indeed, in whom is no guile."

October 9

Have for some days been much indispo[...] has perhaps prevented me from hearing [...] great preaching, some Baptist Ministers were in the Village yesterday, two of them call'd on me, but I was too sick to go with them to the Lord's house. [...] was what grieved me a little, but I believe [...] the best.

October 13

Have been meditating on that part of the Sacred Volume where it tells of the miracle of the Loaves and Fish's.—Matthew 14.—19th and 20th Verses.— "And he commanded the multitude to sit down on the grass, and took the five loaves, and the two fishes, and looking up to heaven, he blessed, and brake, and gave the loaves to his disciples, and the disciples to the multitude. And they did all eat, and were filled, and they took up of the fragments that remained twelve baskets full."—

I am perhaps led to think with the celebrated, but unfortunate Dr. Dodd, on this subject,—that the Loaves, and fishes, grew, and multiplied imperceptably in the hands of the multitude, even while they were in the very act of eating, and while they perceived it not.—be it any way that it would, it was altogether marvelous!—It is frequently said in this our day, that miracles have ceased; but let us consider a while, let us consider this globe we live on, which is but a little part of the Universe, but a little part of that *great whole*, which has been drawn out, and created by a master's hand.—let us meditate a little, and surely we cannot but confess, that it is *all* wonderful, and marvelous in our eyes.—in each successive day we might behold somewhat that is miraculous, were we sufficiently to meditate on all that [...] before us, for "The heavens declare the glory of God and the firmament sheweth his handy work."—[...]

incomprehensible and wonderful to us is the growth of [ve]getation, and the multiplication, and encrease of [a sin]gle seed put into the earth!—and also the gro[wth and in]crease of the human species, and other ani[mals the]at cover this terragueous globe.—were we for instance [...] take even a blade of grass, and view it, when it first [...]apace its green head out of the earth, and could we fix [...] attentive gaze on it, even until it arrived at mat[urity] could not be sensible of its progression, and it [...] grow beneath [...] eye, ready to scatter its seed around and yet its progression would not have been perceived by us.—and thus too, might we mark the growth of the Oak, the monarch of the wood, or mark the expansion of the flowers that bud, and bloom in our gardens.—The Infant too of a day old, continues growing beneath the eye of a fond Mother without even *her* anxious glance perceiving the rapid progression of size, and the change which each succeeding day produces, but yet, all unperceived, the human plant (if spared) continues to grow, and to expand until it arrives at maturity.—how imperceptable to the eye is the growth of all animals!—How wonderful to us the encrease of grain, and of all nourishment for the support of animal existance!— Surely if we were to look at all these things reflectively, we would say it is the work of the Lord, and altogether incomprehensible, and marvelous in our eyes! perhaps we might be induced to think it quite as wonderful as even the very great miracle which our ever blessed Lord perform'd in the desert, when he fed the multitude, encreasing the number of Loaves and Fishes.—"Who can declare the wonders of the Lord, and all that he doeth for the Children of Men!"

November 20

Have sometimes had some good preaching from the Methodists,—they appear to have a persevering spirit, and will not give up this sinful Village of Port Royal.—oh, that he who governs all things, may yet make some one among his faithful servants, the means of saving grace to these perishing souls!—that they may yet reform from the error of their ways, before the night cometh when no man can work!

December 15

One of the Presbyterian brethren has been with us, he preach'd us a very *great* sermon, and a very *consoling* one, to *Christians*, from Proverbs—the text.—"there is one that sticketh closer than a Brother."—and oh, how thankful did my heart feel [...] it went along with him in his discourse, to my God, and to the preacher for such a sermon!—it was exactly suited to my frame of mind, and exactly suited to such a poor lonely one as myself, who have none but my God to look to, but he is my Father, and my friend!—yea, Jesus is my Friend!—I feel that he is and that he is more to be desired than gold,—yea, than much fine gold!"—I hope the Rev. Mr. Dorman will preach to us again! for I am much pleased with this Presbyterian Brother,—should we not love all, who love the ever blessed Immanuel?—and the Presbyterian is the friend of God!—who can doubt it that hears him preach!

December 20

Having recently perused some beautiful lines, sent me by a Methodist Minister, I have written the following, on the Graves, a momentous subject, and an awful one, and one I frequently meditate on,—it would seem as if our heavenly Master had inspired [...] young Methodist, and myself, to write on the same subject.—oh, I trust we have both been inspired to write under the influence of the same spirit!—The holy Spirit of God!—perhaps I am not quite at liberty to copy his production—My stanzas flowing from my head, and heart, such as they are,—are these, and address'd to my Methodist Brother. —

The Grave

Faith, Hope, and Love, they brightly beam,
Shedding their radiance o'er thy song;
And deep my spirit drinks the theme,
As thy soft numbers float along.

An awful theme! the dark, cold Grave!
Ah!—who may all the myst'ry tell?
And who may all its terror brave
Ere yet they in its confines dwell?

No traveler has made return,
To tell us of that narrow place;
For they who once have gone the bourne,
Cheer not again our earthly race.

But when this worldly dream is o'er,
We know the Body mould'ring lies;
The bosom cold, now heaves no more,
The heart once sensate, no more sighs!

Here all is still!—but is this all?
To moulder thus in Earth's dark womb?
Ah no!—there is a Trump shall call,
And break the Sabbath of the Tomb!

• 1823 •

{....}before the foundation of the World."

January 26

On this day, the holy day of St. John the Evangelist, when the votaries of worldly pleasure sought for happiness in the festive halls of dissipation, while they were still preparing to protract their joys until the midnight hour, "droping adours, droping wine," when musick should float on the ear, and the song of joy resound in the Village, filling its festive halls with mirth, and "turbulence unholy," when the gay daughters of vanity were preparing their most dazzling attire, that they might burst in a blaze of beauty on the flattering admirers at the nocturnal hour,—even then it was, at such an hour, and such a season, that I sought the Chamber of Death, the mourners sat around, they wept, and were sad, for Death was in that room, and the stillness of Death was there;—there was a silent language which seem'd to say,—tread softly, nor disturb the ashes of the dead,—and I *did* tread soft, and light, as I approach'd the bed where lay the inanimate clay,—the winding sheet, the spotless veil that shrouded it, was gently lifted,—and I beheld,—oh, what a sight was there!—the pallid hue of Death sat on the countenance,—the change in a few short hours had been great, and scarsely to be recognized were the features of her who had been in the circle of my social acquaintance.—ah, thought I, such must *I too* one day appear, gastly, and loathsome, when death has claim'd his prey!—the day will come (and for aught I know, may not be far distant) when these pliant limbs, now nerved with health, and strength, elastic and rapid in their movements, will become stiff, cold, and motionless, by the destroyer *Death*,—methinks the fearful object before me speaks a language to my sensitive mind,—even from the dead methinks I hear a voice that says,—Judith prepare thee [to] die!—and shall I not be prepared for the heavenly Bridegroom?—I who have no earthly tie!—forbid it thou great Immanuel—forbid it the triune God!—oh aid me to keep my lamp ready trim'd! let me be the wise Virgin, all in readiness for the heavenly Bridegroom, so shall I win on bouyant step my airy way, seeking the bosom of my Father, and my God!—I shall bear my conquering palm, I shall welcome the friends that may [...]—perhaps I may welcome my dear Missionary friend {....}[70] his loving kindness to me!—then blest with "my Saviour's love, my [Saviour's] smile." what shall I have to dread? "For I am persuaded, that neither

---

[70]Order reconstructed.

death, nor Life, nor angels nor principalities, nor powers nor things present, nor things to come.—nor height, nor depth, nor any other creature, shall be able to separate us from the love of God, which is in Christ Jesus, our Lord."—yes, I feel that he is precious to my soul; and tho I may have on earth but few friends; yet I Have one in heaven,—one that is worth every other!—I love to think that there is one safe hiding place, one quiet harbour, where my Anchor is cast.

January 29

Have just received a very spiritual, and friendly Letter, from my friend Mr. K—I consider his Letters, and those of H, B, P, M.—amongst the number of blessings which a kind Providence graciously deals out to me, all unworthy as I am, for, of myself, I am nothing,—and at the *best*, I am even then, "less than the least."—but though "less than the least," I will yet trust that he who considers "the Lilies of the field," also considers *me*,—and he by whom not even one sparrow is forgotten; shall he not also remember me?—he himself hath said, "even the very hairs of your head are number'd"—Oh, then let me trust in the Lord and believe that he considers me!—even me his lowly handmaid!—and oh, that I might improve every occasion, and every offer'd privilege!—I would that I could feel myself growing every day in grace!—feel more, and more the growth of Love in my heart!—but alas, I but too often find myself dull, and languid, as if wanting an incentive to action!—again, and again do I ask myself, from whence can this proceed?—again, and again, do I question myself,—is my faith too weak?—or is it owing to my peculiar situation in this Village of Port-Royal, where sin abounds, and where every attempt in the Christian cause is unavailing?—ah me!—when I find that my feeble attempts to serve my divine Redeemer are all unsuccessful, and that I have to endure in this place, a series of low, and petty persecutions, my heart seems to die within me—and I am often tempted to ask myself,—am I indeed the Child of God, that [...] should be thus?—but away with these doubts, and fears! [...] [e]ven now, it may be, that my worthless name is inscribed [...] the "Lamb's book of Life," and the day fast approaching [...] through the Mediation of my Saviour, I may be pur[e] to join the lovely host of glorify'd spirits that surround [thy] Throne of Love rejoicing,—how my hopes rise within me at the thought!—"Let" us exult in Hope, and all shall yet be [...]—What a comfort it is to the Christian that there is One in Heaven who knows the desires of the heart, and that though reviled, and persecuted here on earth, there is yet a reward laid up in reversion for those who love God!—He hath said, even *He the blessed, and divine Redeemer* himself hath said,—"Fear not, little flock; for it is your Father's good pleasure to give you the kingdom."—The *Word*, the *Promise of Jehovah* is immutable!

February 10

The Rev. Mr. Dorman of the Presbyterian Church, has again been preaching to us,—yesterday he gave us two Sermons, they were powerful discourses, and awful were the very affecting warnings convey'd in them!— methought I sensibly felt my short comings,—felt how feeble, how imperfect a Being I am!—oh for more holiness of heart!

March 13

Heard yesterday two eloquent, and spiritual discourses from Davis, the young Methodist Brother, perhaps the last we shall hear from him in this place.—Surely the spirit of the Lord is on him!—and I trust his blessing too!— he has my prayers for his welfare in whatever corner of the vineyard he may be destin'd to preach the glorious Gospel of Christ.

April 14

A Letter just handed me!—Harriet Mason, the friend I so much valued, is gone "the bourne from which no traveler returneth."—Harriet, will no more be seen in the Flesh, she has departed in her loveliness, adorn'd as she was, with Christian graces,—But why lament departed friends"—and why lament them when they depart in Jesus?—yet a little while, and I may be where Harriet is.— The lovely saint has taken her upward flight, she has ascended to *her* Father, and *my* Father, and I will think she is waiting me on "a shore of better promise."— oh, for daily renewals of grace, that I, like her, may persevere unto the end, and my last departing steps, mark the beauty, and truth, of the Christian Religion, and [...] forth the glories of the Redeemers Cross.—"Let me die the death of [...] righteous, and let my last end be like hers."—"yea blessed are they [...] die in the Lord."—I loved Harriet, dearly loved her! there was [...] what peculiar in our friendship, we were entirely unknown to [...] other, until an introduction from a holy Man of God brought us [...]ed, he introduced us to each other, and that just when he was {...} leave the Shores of America forever.—oh, it seem'd as if it had been a rich Legacy which he left behind, to cheer us two, when he was gone—as if like Elijah, he had dropt his mantle behind, and bequeath'd a parting blessing.—and it was a blessing!—for who may say, how sweet is a Christian friendship,—that Oneness in Christ, which Christians feel when they love one another, and thus in doing so, obey one of the Saviour's last parting commands,

when he said,—"A new commandment I give unto you, that ye love one
another; as I have loved you, that ye also love one another."—Surely our
favorite Andrus, who seem'd to endeavour in all things, to follow the Saviour's
track, must have thought of this, when he at parting introduced Harriet, and
myself to the friendship of each other.—Well, my two spiritual favorites are
now *both* gone!—Joseph R. Andrus, and Harriet B, PP, Mason, are doubtless
now in the presence of their *Beloved.* for I believe it was given to each one of
them to say,—"This is my beloved, and this is my friend, O daughters of
Jerusalem."—yea, they had both found that there "Is One that sticketh closer
than a Brother,"—But they have now gone to receive the reward of all their
Faith, and Love,—doubtless they are now in the presence of God forever, for,
they both shone; each in their proper sphere, as bright examples, during their
short probation here on Earth.—and now they are receiving the rich reward laid
up in reversion for those who love the Lord.—Methinks I behold Harriet, she
who was on Earth the lovely Matron, but now in heaven the glorified Saint,
methinks I see her, with her Cherubic offspring, [...] proceeded her, they now
surround the Throne of Love rejoicing,—Harriet [...] been a Mother, and seen
two lovely infants depart before her, the one by a stroke of lightening, the other,
by sickness, but like faithful Abraham, she could yield them to her God without
a murmur,—each time she could say,—"Thy will, and not mind be done"—and
when she was herself called to follow them, she still said, "all was best that
came from the hand of our heavenly Father"—who may doubt but that she loved
God supremely, she now has her reward?—and how rich the reward of Faith,
and Love, is [...] beyond the conception of the human mind, but surely it is one
part of [...] joy, to be reunited to her sweet Babes, who had got home to glory
but a little before her, and to behold them little angels of light, sparkling [...] the
radiance of Jehovah's Throne,—ah, who may speak the joy!—[...] narrow are
the bounds of finite comprehension!—"eye hath not seen, [...] ear heard, neither
have enter'd into the heart of Man, the things which [God] hath prepared for
them that love him."—our comprehensions are imper[fect] here, but in that
heaven to which the Christian aspires, *all* is perfect,—comprehension enlarged,
and the feelings more exquisitely attuned to happ[...]—we shall not feel, and
understand in *part.*—we shall not see as through glass dimly, but the veil will be
removed.

     And we shall feel, and see, and [know]
     All that's but faintly sketch'd below
How imperfect must be our idea of these things, while we groan in [...]
Tabernacle of clay.—but Harriet, her happy spirit is now free from every

incumbrance, she has reach'd the blessed abodes of the "just made perfect," where there is no sin, no sorrow, where every tear is wiped away,—happy beatified Harriet!—may I meet thee on that shore of Better promise, where parting is no more!—even where Jesus is.

Oh, happy Friend! no more to roam,
A pilgrim in this Vale of tears;
Now thou hast gain'd thy long sought home,
Beyond the reach of earth born cares.

Bursting the tenement of Clay,
Thy soul has upward wing'd its flight;
to scenes of everlasting day,
Of endless glory and delight.

Around the glorious Throne above,
Harriet joins the ransom'd host;
And tunes the notes of praise and love,
To Father, Son and Holy Ghost.

April 18

Have been agreeably surprised by a visit from some valuable Christian friends.—Mr. and Mrs. Keech; Mr. and Mrs. Smith.—Mr. Keech has [...] me something to think of, he has advised me to quit this sinful village where it would seem as if there was but little to profit the Christian.—he advises me to go to Washington, where I should move in a situation more suitable.—even now, methinks I hear the words of this excellent Christian, when seriously looking, he exclaim'd—"you are not moving in your sphere!"—I have thought this myself, I think it is wrong for me to stay, and yet with my slender income it seems almost impossible to go.—there can be but one advantage to me in my Christian course in Port Royal,—*some* of these people in their conduct towards me,—in their fault finding [mercy] to keep me humble.—I have every day, lessons of humility, [...] but few privileges.—bowing at the foot of the Cross, I may with [...] truth, confess myself "less than the least."

April 21

Have received notice that Mr. Morrison, the youthful Presbyterian [will] preach to us on Sabbath next,—he gave us two excellent Sermons [...] weeks since, and I am now anticipating a pleasant Sabbath in the [...]—I think the

Presbyterian, a great Preacher, though he is to [appearance] a very young Man.—well, it is God gives the power.—

April 22

An unexpected privilege! Have just been inform'd [that] the Rev. Mr. Jones, an Episcopalian will preach in the Village on [...].—It will glad my heart, to join yet once again in the service [...] of my church.

Friday Morn

A disappointment the Episcopalian did not preach.

Monday Morn

Heard yesterday two very good and very Evangelical sermons from the Rev. Mr. Morrison, the young Presbyterian, his subjects are well adapted and well calculated to do good in Port Royal, if those who are the hearers, would also, be the doers of the word, but alas how very few ever of those who profess to be followers of the glorious Redeemer live up to their privileges—I feel my shortcomings—but it would seem as if I could do nothing in this Village, where I so often feel the persecutions of those who do not *think* and *feel* as I do—often when I mix in with society here, and afterwards remember somewhat that I have said or done, I blush for having acted, or spoken so, and yet I should have blush'd for myself, had I spoken, or acted otherwise. Mr. Morrison, yesterday, beautifully, and faithfully, set forth the value of the never dying soul, and the glorious and lovely plan of salvation—though apparently quite a Youth, he is yet, in my opinion a great Preacher—a faithful ambassador, for his heavenly Master, and a bold soldier in the glorious cause of our beloved Emmanuel! This youthful Preacher appears to be well taught, both of *God* and *Man*, for he has a plain, and at the same time, elegant flow of language, the holy spirit seems to rest upon him, while he shows forth the truth and beauty of divine things.—In the evening of yesterday, while he was yet exhorting, and admonishing, even then there came a summons to some in the congregation, to repair to the chamber of *Death*—awful summons!—and it was even then, when the youthful preacher was entreating his hearers to seek an interest in their soul's salvation, through the merits of a crucified Jesus—well Port-Royal has solemn warnings, and repeated calls—repeated and awful!

Monday Eve

Have just heard Mr. Morison again, he has preach'd on the late mournful event, and pray'd;—nothing could be more appropriate than his prayers, and his Sermon, he seems to leave nothing unsaid, that could be said.—May this dispensation of divine providence in the death of a promising inhabitant, be sanctified to the surviving relatives of the deceased, and to this Village where sin abounds,—"Afflictions oft, are angels sent on embassies of love!"

July 24

Have been confined for nearly three months to my House, with bodily indisposition, and have been prevented by debility and disagreeable feelings from attending to this my Note-Book. —

July 30

Have again had the exquisite delight of attending the sanctuary of God, and hearing the preached word—with much pleasure, and I hope some profit, I have heard the Rev. Mr. Gibson of the Methodist Church, and spent some pleasant moments with him before, and after service, in company with some of the members of his Church, who are I trust the friends of God and also my friends—yes, even in Port Royal there are some kind and gentle spirits, some who appear to estimate the lonely Episcopalian for they seem'd grieved to miss her from her accustomed haunts—the Sanctuary—the Sabbath School—well, she is again restored! the unworthy J.L. is again restored to her usual health and the enjoyment of her usual privileges—again she fills her seat in the Church— again she performs her usual duties at the Sabbath school. and again she is able to take her usual walks—the people of God again greet her in her usual haunts— and she finds to her joy, that there are some even in Port Royal who know how to estimate her—not by all is she the despised Episcopalian.

{....} come time since, heard from [... mem]ber of one denomination of Christians, attack as I thought, another branch of the Christian Church, I could not refrain from feeling much on the occasion, as fearing it might be injurious to the great Redeemer's cause, and dreading lest there should be a reply made by some of the Ministers of the Church which had been attack'd and thus bring on a controversy in the Pulpit, I have ventur'd to address the next one who shall preach here, and have just thrown in his way, my Letter sign'd Anonymous, I have felt the more liberty in doing this, because I am not a member of either of the Church's alluded to, and therefore can not be supposed to plead for any but

the *Universal Church of Christ*—I trust I have been led to this by the Spirit,—I
have written to the Minister, nearly to this effect.—

There is One,—a lonely beam!—she cometh from her secret chambers,
from the watchings of her inmost soul,—a bruised reed she is, and weak, and
tender, but she leaneth on a sure staff, even on the bosom of Jesus, who helpeth
her infirmities, for he knoweth how fragile she is, and remembereth where of
she is made,—yea, it is her beloved Immanuel, her bosom's Lord, that
supporteth her tottering steps, that watcheth her goings out, and her comings in,
and shadoweth her with his heavenly wings of Love,—it is his whispering spirit,
that speaketh to her spirit, at Morn, and Noon, and setting Sun, and even in the
watchings of the Night, biding her be *Holy*, to keep her Lamp ready trim'd, and
burning for that she shall "know neither the day, nor the hour wherein the Son of
Man cometh."—it bideth her in whispers soft and sweet, to be prepared to meet
the heavenly Bridegroom,—there is One,—a lonely beam!—but the Lord careth
for it, he looketh down from heaven upon its,—with his breath he reneweth the
oft times expiring embers,—thus lighting up a fresh, the flame his love had
kindled—he careth for the bruised reed!—Precious Jesus, that should thus take
account of that lonely one in her secret Chambers!—"Guide her oh, thou great
Jehovah!"—thou who knoweth that on Earth she hath none to help her, none to
guide [h]er,—a lonely pilgrim in this vale of tears, she glanceth from [ea]rth to
heaven, and with an eye of faith looketh to *thee alone*, know [...] it is thou "who
tempereth the wind to the shorn Lamb."—no earth[ly] Pastor hath she destin'd
as she is to be attach'd to that lovely [branc]h of the Church below, which now
lieth neglected in this corner of [the vine]yard.—Like some lone Sheep having
no sheep fold to rest in, [...]ith about in the beautiful meadows seeking food, and
nib [...] , and there, in the rich pastures of others.—no earthly Pas[tor...] be!—
but she looketh to the great "Shepherd, and Bishop [...]he!—yea,—"the Lord is
her Shepherd; therefore can she lack [nothing], shall feed her in a green pasture,
and lead her forth be [...]rs of comfort."—a lonely beam!—she is not a
Presbyte[rian], Baptist nor yet a Methodist—no matter for *names*!

[...]is, the [...] knoweth,—and she believing there will be [...] [...]ly in
heaven, loveth *all* that be of *Christ*.—and now she cometh forth from her secret
chambers, from the watchings of her inmost soul, trusting that the spirit of the
Lord leadeth her, and is resting on her,—that spirit so full of love, breathing
peace and good will toward God, and Man,—yea, she cometh forth the friend of
Zion, and of Zion's cause, to entreat a Christian Brother to bear with her, while
she in the Spirit of Christian charity, would respectfuly address him, the holy
messenger of her God!—not as a teacher doth she come,—she professeth not to

be a teacher in Israel. Knowing that *Woman* shines but in her *proper sphere*,— she would not presume to dictate to one far *better* taught than her in divine things,—but thinking that it may be sometimes, that the most enlighten'd Christians though they require not to be *told* of their duty may yet have need to be *reminded* of it.—thinking that this *may* be, she would with all the diffidence of a Female, and with all the humility of a Christian, just point to some beautiful precepts, and passages, and commands of holy writ.—she would do this because she thinketh it is the spirit of God that prompteth her,—the spirit of *Universal Love!*—but first she would with all due difference ask, if it should not seem a strange thing, that there should be dissentions in the Church of Christ when God is *Love?*—she herself would say, that she believeth that all of Religion is sum'd up in that One precious word *Love*—Our ever blessed Lord, ere he departed from Earth, enjoin'd his followers to love one another.—"This is my commandment that ye love one another, as I have loved you."—and how beautiful did he in his memorable Sermon on the Mount enforce Christian forbearance, and Charity, or in other words, *Love!*—various are the passages in that divine discourse, wherever he particularly dwelt on what he appear'd to have so much at heart—Then oh, remember thou, whosoe'er thou art, who hat[h] taken up the Cross! that thy Saviour hath bid thee, when thou persecuted for righteousness sake, to "Rejoice and be exceedin[g...] for great is thy reward in heaven: for so persecuted they [...pro]phets which were before thee."—How beautifuly consistent is [...] on of Jesus in its every part!—dissentions in the Church of [Christ] truly that would seem to be impossible!—St. Paul saith, [...] divided?"—the intelligent mind would answer, nay but [...] his followers be divided?—is *he* not the living head?—the [...]—how exquisitely beautiful are the fourteenth and fifteenth [...] of St. John on this!—the Christian read them with {....}[71] and justifying *all* that will *Look* to *him* and *Live*, binding [...] in heart, and proclaiming Liberty to the Captive.—and [...]that it was *Love*, amazing *Love* which wrought the glorious [...]Then may it be ask'd, "was ever Love like this?"—and if the [...] Saviour could thus manifest his Love, by dying for his enem[ies] much more are *Brethren* bound to Love one another and by so do[ing] evidence that they are bound in the cords of Love to their glorified Redeemer!—There is One,—a lonely Beam! The delighteth much to hear the preached word, and Faith, Hope and Charity are the themes she loveth, and she holdeth it in mind, that the greatest of these is *charity*—having but very, very few opportunities of publicly joining in the beautiful church service of that

---

[71] Order significantly reconstructed.

branch of the Christian church to which she particularly belongeth. she contenteth herself with using the divine Liturgy in private, and thus in her [...] to worship the Lord in the "beauty of holiness."—[...] worship of the Godhead, she holdeth it her duty to join [...] it a glorious privilege to unite with Christians [...] nation, in worshiping the Lord of hosts,—in render [...] holy Trinity,—the ever blessed *Three* in *One* [...] for all Christian denominations, and [...] every [...] here.—May the Lord build up the walls of Zion! [...] "peace within her walls! "—and oh happy day, when [...] of the Lord on Earth, shall rise from the Church militant [...] to the Church triumphant in the skies!—there where Christians of every name shall meet, of all kindred and of every people—there will be but one family in heaven!—"Praised be the name of the Lord, from this time forth forever more."—all praise and Glory to the great *I AM* for the means of Grace, and for the hope of Glory.—so saith the friend of Zion, and of Zions [cause].

December 25

And dost an Almighty arm still support me who am "less than the least"— yes, he takes account of the lonely one in her secret chambers, "He who is the giver of every good, and perfect gift." sees fit that I should again hail the [name] which brings round the day that marks a Saviour's birth [...] was on the 25th day of December that a God, even the Second [...] the Trinity, deign'd to take our nature upon him, and to be cloathed in flesh.—He comes!—let every knee be bent,—the lovely Babe of Bethleham, claims the homage of every grateful heart.—He comes, the Prince of peace! let all nations bow before him, and acknowledge him Lord of all.—let us worship him {....}

• 1824 •

January 1

And am I spared to see the coming [of] another year?—oh that increasing [...] bring increasing [...] to me, so that I may be [...] work [...] all my Father's will is [...] the Virgins, having my Lamp read trim'd and burning [ ] red, and joying to [...] the heavenly Bridegroom!—[...]dren, panting to be [...] time roll on, {....} there on that happy shore.{....}of the Methodist Church [...] treasure up in my mind his [...] discourse in whi[ch] he pointed out the duty of reading the Scriptures with [...] and [...] our conduct thereby—he commended [...] in the [...] impressive language, may his discourse [...] bless'd [...] profit his hearers!— his [subject] was from the first chapter of St. James, and 25 Verse. "But whoso [...] [...] in the perfect law of liberty."

January 25

Heard yesterday evening a lovely and interesting discourse from the Rev. [...] Methodist Church, it was taken from the I book of Peter, [...] Chapt. and [...], ye holy, for I am holy.—A very humbling theme [...] while I [...] how for short I come to fulfilling this [...] and, but yet I look in faith to him form whom the [...] and cometh; as believing that all things are possible with God, [...] as to obey this mandate, if we earnestly desire it; for I am [...] I that he has never enjoin'd any one thing on us but what is attainable—then let me supplicate him on my bended knees to encrase his work of grace on my heart, until that heart be perfected in love and holiness [...] may I abound in every good work, and my every thought, word, and deed, be found acceptable in his sight; and the end be everlasting life!

{....} my Lungs[72] {....} these brittle tabernacles of Clay {....} sensations!—but it is well that it should be {....} are reminded of the fragility of what is mortal and [...] Eternal duration of the incorruptible.

February 9—

The Rev. Mr. Wilson, of the Methodist Church, preach'd last night at early candle light at Mr. Summersun's, and held a Class meeting. we had a truly interesting time.—at the close of the meeting, a pious [and] amiable Young Lady came forward, and offer'd herself to the Church. when she did this, it was in a way so touching, that it seem'd to produce much excitement of feeling; and

---

[72]This page opens with an extremely fragmented portion.

I though not a Methodist, felt a joy unspeakable,—may the work of grace continue to progress in the heart of my dear young friend; and may the Christian cause spread under whatever name seemeth good unto the Lord.

February 16

Heard the Rev. Mr. Cushen, preach yesterday, from the first Book of Corinthians, the two last verses of the third Chapter.—"Whether Paul, or Apollos, or Cepha[s] . "—it was a handsome, and useful discourse from which much profit might be derived—methinks there is scarsely a Sermon preach'd but what there may be some profit derived. how responsible then are we for the manner in which they are received.—may a Prayer hearing God yet [pour] out his spirit on the Village of Port Royal!—Our Sabbath school seems to [be] improving, we have lately had an acquisition in a Teacher a young Presbyterian who is preparing himself to preach the Gospel.—this young disciple of Christ appears to be zealous in all that can promote the cause of his Lord and [...]ter.— he is the leader at our prayer meetings and is endeavouring to make some amendment in them, he [...] we should all bear a part, I feel a great backwardness towards doing anything.—I have much [...] lament [...] be personaly useful—surely I may say it is my beseting sin.—it would seem as if the fear of doing *wrong* disqualifies me from doing anything.—This must be in some degree owing to weak faith.—was I strong in faith, I should sure [be] able shake of this infirmity of my nature if I may so term it for surely God can of his good pleasure give power to even the feeblest and the last of his creatures— of[ten] I am led to mourn that I am not stronger in the cause of God, thinking that if I [...] more faithful Soldier of the Cross, I should be so filled with the idea of him I ser[ve] [...] be no room left for any fear of the creature.—yea, I humble myself [...] mourning to see how very far short of my duty I come—precious [...] low at thy Cross I would bow myself, and bathe those bleeding feet [...] my tears, praying to be forgiven for all my weakness, and that Thou in [thy] mercy will give me more strength, [hearing] that the desire of my heart is [...] thee— enable me to speak of the things that pertain unto thee, that it [...] to me the friendship of Jesus, and how glorious the privil[ege] [...] to it—give me the power and I, even I the *least* of all [...] graciously there hast dealt with me. will tell how [...] ious friend, is no respecter of persons, but will dra[...] lowly spirit even though they be less than [...] not to take up [....] [happily] {....}[a]ccept of those desire, and [forgive][...] will surely forgive me because he knows it is my desire[...] When I am weak, then am I strong."—Even now I feel [...][none] but God can give, and while retired apart from every h[...]

[...] from the world, in my beloved solitude, I feel moments of exquisite [...]
seem as if I could almost exclaim in the language of a Poet.—

"How happy is the blameless vestal's lot!
The world forgetting, by the world forgot;
Eternal sun-shine at the spotless mind!
Each prayer accepted, and each wish resign'd;
Labour, and rest, that equal periods keep.
Obedient slumbers that can wake and weep,
Desires composed, affections ever even,
Teras that delight, and sighs that waft to heaven.
Grace shines around her with serenest beams
And whispering angels, prompt her golden dreams,
For her the unfading rose of Dead blooms,
And wings of seraphs shed divine perfumes"—

Yea,—very sweet are the hours devoted in solitude to my God!—but this must
not be always,—my heavenly father demands something more of his poor,
weak, and tempted Child and though seclusion suits well with the dis[...] of one
who feels herself not a being of this world, having placed her [hopes], and desire
far beyond it, yet even in this world which she sometimes [delights] to be shut
out from, she knows that she has a part to perform,—[...] knows that she must be
up, and a doing,—Then oh my Father, and my God, bless me,—oh bless with
daily renewals of thy grace, her who would in *every way* be devoted to thee.—
give her strength to take up, and bear the cross, and amidst every
discouragement, enable her by thy power, to glorify thy cause,—oh thou whom
her soul loveth!

February 17

A Repertory just handed me, in it I have read an {....} fragment selected
from some of the papers of the departed *Andrus*,—[...] feelings not to be
described I have instantly recognised his style,—his well remember'd
expression,—his sentiments, and opinions,—all, all are familiar!—it is presented
to the public, just in the manner that it should [be]—how affecting are the half
finish'd sentences!—the broken periods of [him] who now wears "a Crown of
Life"—dear Andrus!—now he has reciev'd [the] need of all his worth!—now he
wears his brilliant Crown, the [...] [ard] of Faith, and Love, and patient
persevering in well-doing!—[thought] while I read the precious fragment it
seem'd to urge me on, [...] relating me a fresh to a persevere to the end.—
Andrus speaks!—even [from the] Grave!—"Nostrebor" has well said in his

preface to these remarks, [...] hardly fail to leave some impression especially if read in [...] writer. "—there is *One* who has read them with many [...] writer."— there is *One* who hopes to meet him departed [ ] of better promise,"—weak, and insufficient [...] she would not for [...] give [...] she beholds in fait[h] {....}a blessed immortality—"a Crown of Life"—her eye glances from Earth and in Faith beholds the Crown—she stretchs forth her arm to reach the Father, I stretch mine arms to thee, no other help have I!

February 26

Heard some good Preaching from the Rev. Mr. Cushen, he gave [...] yesterday two good discourses [...] one in the morning the other in the evening—may he [...] bless'd to the profit of the hearers!

March 8

Have just received a Letter by Post, from my [...] friend, Mr. K—at length he [...] agreeing with me in the expediency of the [...] Colonisation—I myself have always look'd on faith to the perfecting of the [...] and am now quite [sanguine]—it appears to me that the attempt will succeed—[...] it *must* succeed, for it is assured by the *cause of God*—What though there may be some, who may act on [...] political principle of aiding national [interest] [...] *some* [...] not having the interest of the ever adorable Redeemer in view—yet shall the advocate for Immanuel's cause, be dismay'd at this, as thinking [...] me will not be bless'd, because God is not the primary motive?—[...] no! not our hopes be cast down for this!—we will cast a retrospective glance to [...] ages,—we will look nearer home, and view the *present*—in the times [that] past, as well as in the times that are *present*, do we not behold our God [...] in mystery, and carrying on his glorious operations by means incomprehensible to the finite mind?—ofttimes do we observe unworthy agents elected and made subservient to carry on his meritorious purposes,—we behold in the history of nations *ungodly warrior, ungodly Statesmen*, doing the work of God, with [...] *willing to do it for God*—the cause is blest, though never [...] the agents, [...]—unblest they must remain, [...] the living God, [...] on the *motive* alone for *them*, the individual blessing depend [...] but the subject may be [...] again, in another point of view—if, as [...] there should be *some* who act on the cold, and worldly principle of nation[...] and have not God in all their thoughts—yet we do know that others [...] nobler in others—and it is to be hoped that there [...] on nobler motives—friends of God—and friends of [...] been the means, and it is to be hoped there are some that [...] *are* the means of a [...] kingdom, and who are they that are now surrounding Jehovah's Throne crown'd with immortal glory?—even they, those brilliant worthees [...] their Father. [...] kindred, and friends and pleasant home, have seal'd with their lives, the truth, and dignity of their motives—and now clad in white, with palm of victory in their hands—these rest from labours—and bless [...] blest are agents such as these! for to such the promises given, {....} the bright reward, surely we may reasonably suppose, that such as these have drawn down [...] blessing not only on *themselves*, but *most assuredly* a blessing on the [...] also,—we will not think that Jehovah would permit a waste of [...] valuable Men—we wilt not think a [...]—a [...] and a [...] have bled in vain.—oh now glory shall spring [...] thee [...]!—yet a little while, and Africa shall shake [...] the fetters of superstition shall drop, and she *shall be great*, [...] in [li]berty of the everlasting gospel,—free in the unsearchable rich's of Chris[t] then shall her night be turn'd into day, "and the Desert shall rejoice, and [b]lossom like the Rose."—then shall the songs of Zion abound, and Echo bear [...] notes around, 'til other heathen lands shall catch the triumphant [...] well please [...] "the glad tidings of great joy."—yea, it [...] be dest[ined] on some other darken'd {....} now carrying on a great work—it may be, that the time is fast approac[hing]—nay even dawn'd, when the *Father* will give to the *Son*, "the Heathen for [his] inheritance, and the uttermost parts of the Earth for his possession."—May [...] and many more, who are now sojourners, and pilgrims, in this vale of tears, [...] wearing crowns of glory, when the fulfilment of this shall come.—beyond [...] azure sky, may we in the presence of *God the Father*—God the Son, and [God] the *Holy Ghost*, look on, with all the glorified Spirits, from on [high] and wonder and rejoice, and adore.—"Glory be to God in the highest, [and] on Earth peace, good will towards men."

March 19

Had an interesting prayer meeting last night, [...] early candlelight, as usual at Mr. Summersun's—the youthful Presbyterian spoke and pray'd, as usual, with much liberty, he has early enlisted [...] banners of Jesus; and appears to be a shining Christian—he is a real acquisition to us in our Prayers meetings, and Sabbath school.

March 22

Have this day written to my Agent [...] Bank, to offer on my account, next month, out of my dividend then [...] thirty dollars for the Missionary Institution, in the Episcopal Church, [me]thinks [...] my heavenly Father, for enabling me to

make this [ ] he put his blessing upon it!—praised be his holy name, [...]
[precious] dealings with me; his poor un[worthy] creature!—

{....} return'd from the Sanctuary, and praised be the [...] Lord [...]
comfortable discourse I there heard, delivered [...] [Presbyterian Brother] his
text from the Epistle of St. John, the 3d verse of the [...] Chapter. "And every
Man that hath his hope etc.. seem'd lifted [...] myself while I heard the
Christian's hope so well [d]efined—yea, verily, every other hope may prove
fallacious but this [...] on [...] sure, and *steadfast*—and oh I would not each [...]
precious *hope* [...] on the [...] sufferings and death of [...] all that the world calls
rich, and great [...]

Monday Morn.

Heard last night at early candle light in the Church a [...] and well
delivered exhortation from the [...] Mr. [...] [...] makes this second time he has
spoken to us extemporaneously—surely [...] is with him; and give him power!—
[it is truly] interesting to hear [...] with such liberty of the things of God, this
young [...] of Cross appears truly to be arm'd with strength from above—[...] of
God, as it doubtless wilt, ever rest upon him and [...] and knowledge [...] grown
in grace!

May 9

Heard yesterday a sermon that pleased me well, spoke the Rev. Dr. White
one of the Methodists lately come to preach in this place.—his Text was from
the 13th chapter of the Revelations of St. John.—8th Verse—"The Lamb [...]
from the foundation of the world"—Even the most illiterate Preach[er...] to fix
my attention and awaken and interest all the [....] the divine Redeemer [....] in
all {....} was slain, but lives again to intercede for me!

May 12

There is one, who not many days since, proposed to me to write to [...]
and to write on that wonderful theme, the Godhead, he wishing to have some of
my views on the subject, it being one which his sceptical mind could not
embrace because he could not comprehend.—oh, the pride of the human heart,
when not regenerated by the enlightening grace of God!—it is this light which
cometh from above, even the divine influences of the holy Ghost proceeding
from the Father, and the Son, which alone gives us to know our own
insufficiency, and to discern how very limited are, the bounds of finite
comp[rehension].—Proud Man!—and didst thou apply to a fellow worm like thy

self, to unveil this hidden mystery?—who art thou?—and who am I, and who is that presuming mortal who with imperfect power shall dare attempt to search into the deep, and hidden things of God, and essay to lift the impenetrable veil of Deity?—and yet oh, Man! I would say to thee, that though we may not with our feeble powers uplift the veil, yet enough of it is withdrawn, to discover to us the glories of the Triune God, the incomprehensible *three in One.*—yea, verily, there is light enough given us even now, in this our feeble, and imperfect state of comprehension to enable us to discern in *part,* and it is a glorious privilege to wait on the Lord in patient Hope, nothing doubting, when he shall his own good time, reveal himself fully unto us, without a veil between, when we shall behold him not dimly, and as through a glass darkly, but we shall see our God as he is, even face to face—then in that good time of the Lord shall our powers be enlarged, and our state so perfected as to enable us to behold the full blaze of Deity.—But this hope of a more intimate, and perfected knowledge of the Godhead can only be give (I conceive) to the Christian believer to one who looks for the fruition of Hope, and the completion of Love through Faith in the merits, and mediation of the Son of God [...] is blessed hope, I [...] can only be given to us, when we [...] spirit of God, witnessing with our spirits, that we are the Children of God—that is when God the Holy Ghost, witness's that God the Father has accepted us through the merits of God the son, and when we having this witness, honor the son, and the blessed spirit, even as we honor the Father—Having therefore this witness abiding in us, we are taught to believe all things and hope all things through him who hath loved us, and given himself a ransom for many,—through him we know that there is a way to peace, yea, even in this Vale of tears, where there is a constant warfare between the flesh, and the spirit, there is yet a way to peace.—I am the way, [the] Truth, and the Life; saith our ever blessed Lord.—there is then a peace, a joy [...] believing which passeth all understanding, even in this our state of trial—but oh, for the peace, the joy prepared for those who love the Lord, when they may conceive the smallest part?—and in that perfected state we have good reason to be made capable of comprehending all things—even the glorious Godhead, ever adorable Trinity, shall then be fully made known to us—But even now in this our probationary state, there is light enough reveal'd to us, to cause us to wonder, and adore the divine Essence, in all his glorious attributes—the light of his holy spirit discovers to us the "Way, and the Truth, and the Life."—he hath given us his own holy word to shew us a standard whereby we may [...] and compare ourselves—for All scripture is given by inspiration of God and profitable for doctrine, for reproof, for correction, for instruction in righteousness {....}

[us] then search the scriptures with diligent prayer, so may the Lord by his Holy spirit give us the hearing ear, and the understanding heart, so may we know the things that shall make for our everlasting peace, and so may we comprehend enough of the Sacred records as may enable us to *believe*, and *embrace* the *whole*. We grow on knowledge; also grow in grace; Faith and Love thus in righteousness, abounding in every good work, to the glory, and honor of God.— and now, oh proud hearted, doubting Man! having pointed thee to the sacred oracles of God himself, if still thy mind is sceptic on this so glorious theme, the Unity of the God-head—the *three in One*—say then, admitting that thou cannot, or will not believe this so wonderful Truth, because it cannot be comprehended by thee, that I know not how we are bound to comprehend all that we believe— does not every day's experience of the powers of the great God of the Universe prove to us that we with our feeble powers of capacity *cannot*—can we understand the wonderful works of Creation daily opperating before our eyes?— let us begin with the vegetative tribe, from the tender blade of grass just shooting its green head above the soil, and growing, and maturing, until it scatters its fruitful seed around,—for the majestic Oak, first shewing itself a little leafy tendril, then growing and maturing, until its lofty boughs overshadow our heads, and its fruitful honors are scatter'd on the ground, that other Oaks, the pride of the Forest may be again produced, a shade for Man and Beast—but who may even count all the wonders of Flowers, springing up, and growing, and buding, and blooming and maturing before our eyes, all produced by the great Author of Nature, but we know not how—we believe, are obliged by optical demonstration [...] these things *are*, but we know not how they are, we do not *comprehend* them.—From the vegetative, we might go to the Brute creation— not only to the Brute Creation, but to the Feather'd creation, the Fowl's of the air, and descend from them, to the Reptile, and Insect tribes.—these are all of them produced by a Master's hand—we know that they *are*., but we do not know *how* they are,—we do not *comprehend* them.—we are obliged to believe that which is so wonderful as to be far beyond the feeble powers of our comprehension.—we believe that we ourselves [...] we are obliged to believe it, we *know* that it cannot admit of a doubt, and we know still more we know that we have a vital principle within us which acts upon the body.—that is we know for we *feel* that we have a Body, and a Soul, acting one upon the other.—we do know that we are "fearfuly, and wonderfuly made." but we do not know *how*, we cannot *comprehend* it.—we only know that it is in god "we live, and move, and have our being."—he hath given to each one of us a soul, and a Body, these *two* act in union in each individual, we believe this, which we are obliged to do,

and that o without *comprehending* it.—may we not very easily believe the Union of *Three in One*, in the *Godhead*? we can no more comprehend the *one* than the *other*—methinks then that we might easily believe *three Persons* being *One God* in the holy Trinity, w hen we know of a certainty, how very limited are the bounds of Finite comprehension—how unlimited, how unbounded the power of Infinite, and Uncreated Excellence,—having these views, it only remains for us to know that our conceptions are too weak whilst we are yet in this imperfect state of existence to comprehend fully what is exalted so far above us.—and methinks the mystery in which it is enwrapt, should even fill us with a greater degree of reverence of the Deity who is so glorious, cloath'd as he is in majesty, and power,—[...] ways are past finding out,—[...] we should make our inability of comprehension a ground of unbelief when we reflect on the weakness of our comprehensive faculties.—[...] mention'd some instances, out of many, of the wonderful operations of the God of nature that cannot be in any way accounted for by the narrow limits of human wisdom—I will now for a moment glance a little at the inventions of the human mind, and descend even to the works of the Creature, we are offtimes, struck with amazement at the ingenuity even of a Fellow mortal, who Genius and acquirements, far transcend our own, and whose person we have never beheld it may be, that this person may by very great genius, and acquirement, produce some invention, or some Art, that we ourselves cannot account for, not understanding the principle of [...],—when this occurs, as it often does, do we ever for a moment doubt the existence of this person because we have never seen him, and because he is superior to us, and different from us in so things?—never doubt of his performance only because we do not comprehend it assuredly not—we neither doubt the existence of the Art, or the Artist—There are very few [...] not any one of us, that can boast of having gone round the whole circle of Arts, and Sciences; there are therefore very many productions of art, and genius, that are undefinable to us, and some of them [...] produce effects that add to our comforts, without our understanding even in the least degree the cause—we nevertheless are not *incredulous* for we are deriving benefits from the effects of this—Thus it is that again, and again, we are obliged to believe what we cannot comprehend.—we must know this by every day's experience—Oh, let us then implicitly believe in the Deity, the great, indivisible *three* in *One*, and never on the weakness of our comprehension, ground out unbelief we have no excuse for not believing—Let us be thankful that [...] in light of Reason, the God of the Universe hath given us his own [...] word, and the teachings of his own holy spirit, to shed light on the way that leadeth to heaven, and to everlasting life—oh, the Christian has joyfuly hails this light which discovers so much of the Deity, as to fill the mind with fervent adoration, and reverential [...] be thankful that the God of the Universe hath given us light enough to discern our way to heaven, and to fix our hearts on him the [...] good—let us receive with thankful humility what he in mercy gives, and be content that he should withhold from our view, what it might be good, that we in our imperfect state should not comprehend—had our first Mother been content with the light of that knowledge—God had given her, she had not sought for that which he in wisdom had deny'd.—it was this insatiable thirst for knowing what her Maker knew it was not good for her happiness that she should know which caused her to disobey a possitive command.—she eat of the forbidden fruit, and fell!—Then let us who are taught of the Spirit, be content that the great Jehovah hath set his bounds to our comprehensions whilst we are yet in our imperfect state,—let us believe that all his schemes with nicest art are plan'd—what a wonderful plan hath he given us in the most glorious one of all—the plan of Salvation through the merits of the great [atonement]—how may we ever humble ourselves enough for this, and for every other gift divinely bestow'd on us, by the giver of every good and perfect gift.—our highest strains of praise, and thanksgiving and adoration come very far short of what we owe, then let us throw ourselves on the merits of a Saviour, for his sake, our feeble offerings of praise, and Love, and thanks will be received.—Oh that our thoughts might be continualy elevated towards Our great Creator, looking to the time when we shall have a more intimate knowledge of him,—when he shall be prepared to meet the full blaze of Deity!—The Christian waits in patient hope, nothing doubting, the coming of the Lord, when *God the Father, God the Son,* and *God the Holy Ghost,*'s all be fully reveal'd in all the wonderful, and matchless glory of the *God head.*

May 25
  Heard yesterday a good Sermon from Doc. Sommerville one of the Baptist Brethren;—The giving way of the galleries in the Church, caused an alarm, and confusion, in the midst of the discourse, we were obliged to quit the Church, so great was the danger, but we heard the doctor finish his excellent Sermon in the Room of a private house.—Our ill fated Church has become now so dangerous as to prevent the services of Religion being perform'd there.— Great was the confusion within its walls on the last Sabbath whilst yet the Sermon was going on; the interp[...] hand of providence alone prevented nay unfortunate accident—for my part, I think I can say that my heart at that moment of personal danger, [...] stay'd on the Lord.

June 8

Heard yesterday, an interesting, and affecting discourse from the Rev. Mr. White of the Methodist Church—

June 28

Last night being Sabbath night, our young friend Mr. Pierson, exhorted at early Candle light to a large congregation.—it is wonderful the strength and boldness the Lord gives to this youthful disciple—[modest] and unassuming he is yet not afraid, nor ashamed, to declare the whole counsel of God, to a whole host of Sinners.—beautifuly does he ex[...] and dwell on the truth as it is in Christ Jesus.—methinks while it is highly interesting, it is yet quite awful, to behold one so young in the midst of a large assembly, mostly composed of sinners, some of whose heads seem blossoming for the grave, to behold him, and to hear him, exhorting, warning and entreating them, and placing before them Life, and Death,—the horrors of Hell, and the joys of Heaven.—yea, it seemeth as if the young Presbyterian knowing therefore the terror of the Lord"he would " persuade men"—and O, that the might indeed persuade the, old, and young, all that hear him who are yet out of the ark of safety, to be "reconciled to God"—and may Saints of the Lord too, be reminded that they must be up and [adoring] they must work while it is yet call'd to day!—may Our cry be to the Lord increase our faith, increase our love, and zeal!

July 5

Yesterday, Sabbath day, we had a powerful, and very affecting discourse from the Rev. Mr. White, the Methodist.—he preach'd from the first verse of the fourth Chapter of Hebrews, "let us therefore fear, lest a [promise] being left us of entering into his rest, etc.—faithful to his trust, he delivers the message of his Lord and master, speaking forth the words of truth and soberness, and *many* might have trembled under the sound of his voice for verily it was a Sermon well calculated to arouse the feelings of both Saint, and Sinner,—and of, when he spoke of the joys of heaven, who might not wish to go along with him there!—My God! give me thy strength to contend for the prize, that I may "so run, that I may obtain"—for thou hast said, "be thou faithful unto death," and I will give thee a crown of life,—[let me hold] in remembrance all thy very precious promises looking to Jesus the author, and finisher of our faith."

July 10

What are we Lord that thou art thus mindful of us.—that though we dost every day sin against thee, yet is thine arm still stretch out towards us?—still dost thou take account of this poor sinful Village,—still dost thou send thy beloved Servants, thy own faithful Embassadors, to preach [...] of Life, with Truth and power,—still dost thou mercifully hold out forgiveness for Port Royal, bidding them to choose Life, or Death.—Turn ye, turn ye, oh, house of Israel! for why will ye die?—Oh my [Father!] thou hast said it that his own word shall not return [...] void may we not then hope in faith, that this people, this little [...] of thy Vineyard will yet be saved with an everlasting [Sal...] *Thou* can'st do *all* things, Save them, oh save them!—[...] the word only, and Port Royal *shall* be heal'd for we do know [...] there is "balm in Gilead,"—there is a *Physician* there,—[...] cry of thin own faithful people, for here, even here, in this un[...] soil thou hast yet, I trust a peculiar people zealous of good [works]—hear them, oh, hear them, while they pray for thee in faith [asking], doubting and wait thine own time, and thine own seasons, surely the time will come, will soon come, when the fleece shall [...] wed with the dew of thy blessing.—when Jesus shall reign omnipotent!—this day I have been led to hope that a blessing would descend, for this day I have heard the word so faithfully preached that it would seem to me as if the Lord would not permit it to return unto him void—surely the great god of glory must have help'd the speaker's mind to day—help'd with truth, with life, with power.—I have felt it good to be this day under the sound of the Gospel, whilst I heard the Rev. Mr. Wilson, preach from [the] eighteenth Verse of the first Chapter of Ephesians, "The eyes of your understanding being enlightened, etc. etc."[73]—The Presbyterian preach'd like one well taught of the Spirit.—and who may doubt but that the spirit of God was resting on him, whilst he was delivering his message to Port Royal.

Sabbath Morn, July 12

Have just return'd from the Sabbath school, and feel refresh'd from having assisted with other Christians, in the performance of a duty.—and am thankful to the Lord [...] having given to the school a teacher so well qualified as our youthful friend Pierson when he prays for the school it appears to be in spirit, and in truth."—may a blessing descend!—

---

[73]For the reader's ease of reference at this point, the "etc. etc." of Ephesians 1:18 reads: "...so that, with the eyes of your heart enlightened, you may know what is the hope to which he has called you, what are the riches of his glorious inheritance among the saints."

July 26

Have had the pleasure of spending another sabbath much to my satisfaction, attended the school as usual, and was accompanied on my return home by my favorite, the young Presbyterian, he is so spiritual that I can almost immagine [...] while I am conversing with him, that he is an ordain'd Minister of God, and notwithstanding his extreme youth, I find it quite profitable to hold sweet converse with him,—oh, it is a sweet privilege to associate with a Religious, and intellectual [...]—my Baptist friend, Miss Timberlake, and another Lady [join'd] us in the Evening.—so that I yesterday spent a very pleasant Sabbath having spiritual society in own house, after the [...] duties of the day was over.—all praises to the great [I Almighty].

August 2

Spent the last Saturday, and the last Sabbath, much to [my] satisfaction, having enjoy'd much of the presence of God, in mingling with the Methodists, and other Christians, at a two day Methodist meeting in this place, and once again with them approach'd my heavenly Father's hallow'd board, and received from their hands [a] sacred memento of a bleeding Saviour's love.—for this high privilege blessed be my great Redeemer's name!—yet blessed be the condescending mercy of a God which permits a feeble worm of the dust like myself to be a partaker of his heavenly love, and thus to receive the rich memorials of it, in the hallow'd cup, and broken bread.—thus to remember that Christ's blood was shed for me!—And now O divine benefactor, thou Saviour of sinners! having renew'd my covenant with thee and in the face of a world again [...] thine, I would pray thee to continue forth thy loving [...] giving me daily renewals of thy love, that so I may live as becomes a follower of thee, having each day "a closer walk with God." until being made fully ripe for the joys of heaven, I shall "drink no more of the fruit of the vine, until that day that I drink it new in the kingdom of God."—O, great God of glory, sanctify me wholly, that I in thy good time, may receive a crown of Life and join the ransom'd around thy throne forever!—

August 9

How uncertain are even our most rational pleasures whilst we are in this temporary state of existence, and the enjoyment of them, [...] fleeting—oh, they are evanescent as the passing cloud, or the [...] beauties of the spangled dewdrop of a May day morn—and, it is [...] that it be so,—our fast fading earthly enjoyments, surely they speak in audible language to the reflective mind, and seem to cry as they rapid pass away, "let your affections on things above, not on things in the earth—I am led into this train of thought by the departure]of our interesting friend, the young Presbyterian, he will be much miss'd in this place by [those] of us who be of Christ, for during his short residence in this neighbourhood he has been our constant, and delightful associate in all our labours of love.—my heart sink within me when as we were conversing together on Saturday evening, he told me he was about to leave us.—he had come perhaps just to tell me of his departure, and say farewell—and now we shall miss him from our accustom'd haunts, no more shall we greet him in our little Sabbath school where he presided so much to our satisfaction.—he will no more bless with religious instruction the class of poor Boys,—he will no more greatly commence, and close our duties at the school by his fervent and pious [...]—and Pierson will no more distribute for us the prize, as we would delighted point him to the most deserving of our Girls.—yes, he is gone!—we shall have him no more at our Sabbath School,—our Prayer meetings, etc. etc.—and I shall no more have his religious, and interesting conversation in my own house, where I have so much delighted in having his society.—but it is well,—set your affections on things above, not on things on the earth."—

Monday Morn-

Yesterday went through the duties of the day as usual, attended Sabbath school, etc. etc.—Our school seem'd dull without the Presbyterian, but I remember'd him at a throne of Grace, while praying for the school, and for all the world, and while I pray'd *especially* for the *friends of Jesus*—often is Pierson, he who has been our fellow labourer, remember'd in my feeble prayers.—it is methinks very sweet at a Throne of Grace, to remember our absent friends and more particularly those who are the friends of our beloved *Immanuel*.

Monday Morn

Yesterday as usual went through the exercises of the [...] attending Sabbath School, etc. etc.—In our Sabbath school a [...] circumstance somewhat singular occur'd soon after the [...] school had open'd, and we had commenced teaching the children, a stranger appeared in the midst of us, bowing respectfully he took his seat, and after some little time offer'd to assist in teaching the Boys, for which office he appear'd well qualified, and in closing the school for us, he address'd the Children [in a] very appropriate and affecting manner and then concluded the whole with a prayer which I hope was heard in heaven, and will be answer'd in due season by a prayer hearing God.—the stranger having thus kindly render'd us his assistance, departed, unknowing, and unknown,—even his *name* unknown, but I trust the Lord sent him to us for good.

September [...]

Had yesterday the infinite satisfaction of attending on [...] Service of my own Church, and responding to the Minister in our divine Liturgy,—The Rev. Mr. Carter, an Episcopalian, preach'd to us, he took his Text from the Psalms of David and gave us a very good discourse,—after preaching he return'd home with me so that I have once again had the pleasure of entertaining in my own house a Minister of that branch of the Christian Church to which I more immediately belong—may the Lord be praised for this, and all his mercies!

October 28

Went out yesterday through the rain to the Sabbath school because some of the Children came and insisted on it—found none of the other teachers there, had a fatiguing time of it as I had all the Children on my own hands to teach, and they were so rude, and bad, that I had need of all my patience.—I sometimes fear that we the teachers do not teach in the right spirit or we should see more fruits of our Labours.—O, our Father! send down thy power from above, give us thy help in this our time of need, that by the influences of thy holy spirit we may be enabled to teach these little ones aright, and at the last day, present them a little flock to Jesus without spot, or blemish.—may we, and they, be found blameless through the justification of him who hath bled for us on Calvary's brown—may we, and they, be enable through the merits of the great attonement to abide the day of his coming, and to stand when he appeareth!

Tuesday Eve

Heard this morning a very good discourse delivered by the Baptist Missionary, the Rev. Mr. Rice, {....}[74] trifling, a [...] especially will he do so, when the gift is acco[...] the sincere good wish's of the artist.—Yes, there is One [...] General LaFayette, and his Son, the best wish's of the Season.—[...] for General LaFayette, may the approaching year, and may [...]ing ones, come fraught with blessings!—his path-way still strew'd with the flowery wreaths of Glory, and a peace descending on him "that passeth all understanding."—so that

---

[74] Order significantly reconstructed.

whether the remainder of his days be spent in America, the dear favor's land of Liberty, or in his own native France, still may he be happy!—blessing, and bless'd, wherever he may be!—and when at length his number'd days have drawn to a close, and the silent Tomb opens ready to receive him, then may he gently fall asleep in the arms of his Redeemer, and wake to raptures in another, and a [brighter] world,—a world of unutterable bliss, and glory!—there to receive from the righteous Judge an "incorruptable crown"—even "A Crown Of Life."[75]—There is One, who from her beloved solitude has been [...]ted thus to invoke blessings on the Man whom the Nation deligh[...] or.—She too, though in the vale of obscurity, unknowing, and [...]own on Earth, has yet the glorious privilege through faith in [...], and mediation of a Saviour, of seeking a Crown of L[...] Lord hath promised to them that love him."—may [...] she may obtain."—then though on Earth she may [...ha]ppiness of beholding La Fayette, the brilliant, and the good, [...] Champion for Liberty, and the defender of the rights of Man! [...]ay she admit the hope of meeting him, and knowing him in hea[...] midst "the Spirits of just men made perfect."—She, this [...] one, delights to give the reins to her immagination, and [...] mind's eye "behold the disembodied spirits of more [...]hours and years,—Heros,—Sages,—Bards, triumphant [...] bright succession.—urging their rapid flight toward [h]eaven of heavens, they receive the dazzling prize, and join [...] and host and swell the adoring song.

December 25

Hail, all hail auspicious, and eventful day which [...] return's reminding us of the advent of our God the Saviour—[W]hat wonderful, and condescending love for a fallen race was on this day manifested! it was for us miserable sinners that we are, it was even for *me*, that a god came down and took on himself the appearance of a creature, and became as it were a new-born Babe, -yea, it was even for me that the lovely Babe of Bethleham, submited to be wrapt in swaddling cloaths, and to lie in a manger!—there was no room for Our Lord in the Inn!—it was for *me* this lovely Babe even God incarna[te] became a Man of sorrows,—Suffer'd—bled,—and died for *me*!—for even worthless *me*, [...] this day came to make a *great* attonement.—[then] hail auspicious day!—Jesus himself draws night.—open my [...] [be the] breathings of the [...][76] thy holy

---

[75] General LaFayette paid a rather celebrated visit to the United States in 1824. With her family ties among influential circles in Washington City, Judith Lomax probably kept abreast of his visit.

[76]This portion is quite fragmented and has been reconstructed considerably.

handmaiden, who well knows that thou art [...] no [...]rings but those of Love, with no treasure, but the rich tr [...] [of] a [d]evoted heart, she would yield thee hers intire, and on [...] thee, so may she bring to the love [Babe of] [...]and rich oblations, but [give more], thankful heart per[...] [...] and holiness—[...] shall my Saviour not despi[...]

December 26

Heard a discourse from the Rev. M[...] was not spiritual, and therefore there was nothing [....] blessed Jesus to feed on, I came away disappointed {....} [f/g]ood.

December 2[8]

{....} the {....} reaching {....} such good from [...] Rev. Mr.—who [...] two days [...] us, spoke quite to the [...], is that this time I have no[...] [...] empty away.

December 30

Had Preaching last night [...] early [...] light at Mr. Dummers [...], from the Rev. M [...], on the Methodist Brethren [...], oh I found it was [...] for me [be] *there* for I seem'd to have a foretaste of heaven, [whilst] with awe-struck, and wrapt attention I listen'd to the truly Evangelical discourse of this eloquent, and apparently [inspired] Embassador of the blessed Jesus.—there was something exquisite[ly] touching even in the [...] of his voice, which gave such [expression] to his words as render'd them truly affecting, [...] indelibely impressive, whilst his beautiful, and pious count[enance] seem'd to beam with the varying feelings of his soul.—methought while he spoke, his eye gently raised upwards, that he seem'd like some wrapt Seraph from the realms of rest, sent by his heavenly Master on holy embassy,—beautifuly did he expound the Scriptures as he discoursed from the fourth verse of the ninth chapter of the Gospel of St. John.—I must work the works of him that sent me, while it is day: the night cometh, when no man can [...]—Even Christians have need to be reminded of this,—what dependant and yet what accountable creatures are we!—Heavenly Father [I] stretch mine arms to thee! do thou assist me to work out my soul[s] salvation, by giving me daily renewals of thy love. so may I by [...] continual operations of thy holy Spirit on my heart, be enable to work {....}

receive him, and though thou art a rude, and worthless [ ]⁷⁷ [ ] manger for
such a guest, yet is there room enough—Then[...] [...] my Saviour come!—lodge
thou in my heart, and even take thou [...] [mine] abode there!—with thee thou
God of my salvation let me be[...] from the world, for the *world* perhaps too
much resembles the inhospitable Inn.—there is no room in the world for the
lovely Babe of Bethleham!—This is a day for *Christians* to rejoice!—"Glory to
God in the highest, and on earth peace, good-will toward men."—Come O, my
Saviour come, draw near to me thou Prince of peace, and take up thine abode in
my heart,—fill up the space in my secret Chambers, and manifest thyself to me,
not as thou dost unto the world,—behold thy lowly hand maid retired far from
the [noise and] revelry of a tumultuous world, she would hold communion with
none but thee.—"Sanctify her through thy truth: thy word is truth." "O righteous
Father, the world hath not known thee; but I ha[ve] known thee."

---

⁷⁷This page, following the two fragmented ones, may or may not follow in
chronological order. The editor assumes that there may be a page or more missing from the
extant copy at this point.

• 1825 •

January 1, 1825[78]

Another year has sped and yet am [...] !—Almighty Father who hast now brought me [...] ning of another year, teach me by the inspirations of [...] spirit to spend to they glory each moment, and each day [...] lengthens out my span on earth,—yea, Lord, and if in thy [Pro]vidence [a]nother year, or many years be added to be probat[ionary] term, may they all be spent to thy glory!—and should [...] see fit that another year may not again dawn on my [...] existence, oh, then when my last fleeting breath shall fa[ll] [...] me into glory, and take me to dwell with thee on high!—[...]

January 26

Have been reading with much satisfaction "Stories Expl[...] of the Church Catechism. By Mrs. Sherwood—Methinks the name of [Sher]wood, should be dear to every Christian, but more particularly [...] episcopalians.—Her Book clearly shews forth the truth of the Epis[copal] belief, and proves that in our Church Catechism, we have Scripture to [...] on throughout the whole of it.

May 1

Have been permited by my heavenly Father to [...] make life payments to the Bible, Prayer Book, and Tract Societies, and also to become a Subscriber of Five dollars per Annum, to the Theological Seminary for educating Pious Young Men to the Ministry of the Episcopal Church.—for this [and] for all the gracious dealings of God [...], I praise his holy [name.]—yea, praised be the Lord, now and forevermore![79]

---

[78]Note that this entire date is legible in Judith Lomax's handwriting. Here, for the obvious reason of the beginning of a new year, she has included the complete date, particularly helpful for this section which is only a fragment of the year of 1825. Unfortunately, this is the only extant portion of the journal for this year.

[79]Virginia Seminary, a Protestant Episcopal Theological Seminary in Alexandria, was founded in 1823 and is still functioning in the late twentieth century.

• 1826 •

{....}commited to its kindred dust.—The Rev. Mr. Willer, of the Presbyterian Church attended on the occasion, and spoke from the twenty fourth Chapter of St. Matthew—his word were well spoken, and in season.[80]

Sabbath Morn.—January 1/1826 [81]

This day brings back the re[...] of another year.—I yet survive! but where may I be ere yet another year has sped?—for which of us poor short-lived mortals may dare to calculate on a year?—nay even on a month, or week?—we dare not count even on a day, or an hour!—weak frail beings that we are in one short fleeting moment the breath of Life may pass away, and a hasty passport—land us on that shore from whence there shall be no return—heavenly Father! so long as thou shalt see good to prolong—my [seanty] span, wilt thou in tender mercy, and for Jesus sake, give me such renewals of thy grace, as may fit me more and more for the company of Saints and Angels! so that cloathed upon by a Saviour's righteousness, I may ripen for thy kingdom and at length be made a partaker in all the glories of it!— [...] this for Jesus sake, who on this his own holy day ascended far above the heavens, and sat down at God's right hand to plead for his guilty creatures—to plead for me!—blessed Jesus, may I indeed believe that thou art even now, pleading my cause with the Father, and that my Sins are cover'd, and my iniquities remember'd no more?—oh, then so shed abroad thy love in my heart, that I may rejoice at they second coming,—may meet with joy unspeakable my Lord in all his glory!—keep me, oh keep me king of kings!—so may I be always read, always prepared to meet the heavenly Bride groom!—"For the master of the house cometh at even, or at midnight or at the cock, or in the morning."—help me by they quickening spirit to "Watch."

Monday Morn

Spent the two last days with a Sister in the *flesh*, one of my *own kindred*, who has unexpectedly visited me.—I trust we are also *one* in *spirit*, she and I trust the Lord was with us three, and that our meeting was for good,—praised be his holy name!

---

[80] Though this portion would probably be in the previous year, there is a considerable gap and this portion is on the same page as the next entry, therefore it is included prior to the January 1 entry rather than appended to the end of the previous year.

[81] This entire date, with the year, is also included in Lomax's handwriting.

Friday

Have spent some happy moments with another friend from Fredericksburg, Mrs. C[...] an interesting, and I should judge a pious Lady!

February 13

Have hard some good preaching from the Presbyterian Brother, the Rev. Mr. Willer, he is to preach [...] every other Sabbath, though not of the same denomination of the Christian Church with myself, yet I hope the Lord will bless him, as the means of grace to this people!

February 16

Have just been writing to a Minister of my own Church and hope my Letter will be answer'd for I highly prize all spiritual help—it is a great thing to me to receive a Letter from a Minister of my own Church, for I always hope to find somewhat in it that may be the means of helping me on in my way to heaven, and cheering my present lonely path-way in a Vale of Tears.—Oh, what happiness was it to me last summer the enjoyment of the high privileges of my Church in Fredericksburg.—a very limited income not affording me the means is all that now prevents it.—but I trust my heavenly Father will do for me in all things what is best, and should it be his pleasure that it should remove to Fredericksburg, he will make my way plain for me to do so.—and should it not be his pleasure, oh, then, may he still continue to me the influences of his holy spirit, giving me even in the poor little desolate Village of Port Royal, that "peace which passeth all understanding." for with the Christian, *God is every where.*—oh, then how much should we in every situation pray for daily renewals of his love!—his spirit abiding with us, and witnessing with our spirits that we are indeed his.—adopted into his family of Love, and heirs to a bright inheritance in heaven!—it is only the holy spirit of God, opperating on our hearts, and sanctifying our affections, that can at any time give us real happiness—bless with this irradiating beam of a heavenly Father's favor; a dreary solitude becomes a bright abode, and we seem prepared for every dispensation for what should we dread if we have peace through the Son of his Love, and a claim to his very precious promises?—"There is One that sticketh closer than a Brother." but ah, me! when I consider what manner of persons we should be, we who have profess'd to have this blessed hope I am startled, and humbled at the remembrance of all my short comings.—the wandering thoughts of my heart, the idle words of my lips—faithful is that warning.—"keep thy heart with all diligence, for out of it are the issues of Life."—and weak and insufficient, as I am of myself, I know that I should be lost after all my strivings, could I not lean on the merits of a Redeemer, depending on fresh supplys from the fountain of his Love.—yea verily, "except the Lord keep the city, the watchman waketh but in vain."—oh, then my blessed Saviour, hide me under the shadow of thy wing, and since I have no righteousness of my own, enwrap me in thine own spotless robe, so may I at thy second coming not be found wanting, but be cloathed on by thee, clad in white—array'd in the wedding garment! and so may I reach "a shore of better promise" where there is no more sin, and no more sorrow, where every tear is dried—the warfare ended, and the prize "a Crown of Life."—may I and *many more*, attain to this high destiny!

I love to write, I love to pour my thoughts on paper, imperfect as are my best thoughts,—alas, my imperfect, and wandering thoughts oft times prove to me, how necessary the admonition of an old, but favorite poet, "Guard well thy thought, our thoughts are heard in heaven."—oh, then for more holiness of heart—may I every day drink deeper, and deeper, of thy precious fountain of Christ's Love, and thus daily renew'd in spirit, be daily ripening for the joys of heaven, and be made more fit to be a partaker of that blessed kingdom!—

February 18

I have been reflecting on the happiness that must be attendant on the faithful Ministers of the Gospel, those who labour diligently in the Lord's vineyard, having been call'd according to his especial purpose to the high destiny of being his Embassadors, to beseech, and persuade poor perishing Sinners, "in Christ's stead" to be "reconciled to God."—what happiness, to be the means of saving perishing souls!—but god is good—some there are, who though they be the least of all the Saints, yet feel and know that there are some great; and glorious privileges permited them, even *I* who am "less than the least," experience a happy privilege, which world's should not tempt me to forego, when humbled at the foot of the cross, I entreat for more grace, that it may love my God more, and serve him better,—yea, it is a precious privilege, to come like Mary, and bathe the Saviour's beloved feet with tears, knowing that in the language of bishop Beveridge, "our very prayers need repentance, our repentance be repented of, and our tears to be wash'd in the blood of Christ."— oh happiness unspeakable, to have that sacred blood with all its healing powers, applied to the heart!—that blood which cleanseth from all sin!—yea, Lord, wash me each day, and renew me in the precious fountain!—there is a balm in Gilead!—And the Christian believer, finds it a great privilege too, to pray for the prosperity of Zion, so that the time may speedily arrive when all the nations of

the Earth shall be bless'd through him, who gave his Life a ransom for many.—
may the set time to favor Zion now be come, and the labourers [...] not few, but
many, for lo, the fields are white!—Oh, I trust that the blessing of the Lord is
even now resting on the Theological Seminary located in Alexandria, to the
Education of pious young Men to the Ministry of the Episcopal Church, so that
many Labourers may be sent forth, who shall return bearing their sheave's with
them!

Good Friday

On this memorable day methinks with an Eye of Faith I behold the
bleeding sacrifice Once made for Sin, on Calvary—great attonement!—oh, how
deep the stains of Sin, since nothing less than the blood of *a God* could wash
them out!—my sins, the sins of a whole world have caused the Saviour's blood
to flow—I have been bought with a price,—a precious ransom has been paid for
me!—how can I sufficiently estimate it?—no work of mine can pay the debt of
love for any one good thought, I can only shew forth my faith, and love, by
yielding myself up to him, who hath died to save me, and pray for daily supplies
of grace, that I may do his will on Earth, as it is in heaven,—and not only to *do*
his *will*, but to be *resign'd* to *all his will*.—his own words, how memorable! "thy
will and not mine be done."—and shall not these expressive, and affecting
words be impress'd on the minds of his faithful followers?—indellibly
impress'd on my heart may they be!—what though his dealings with *some* of us
may seem *strange*, and *past finding out*, yet shall we not think that even *these*
are mercies in disguise, and meant to draw us more closely to him, and that
"beneath a frowning providence he hides a smiling face."—I will trust him! I
will praise him! I will depend on him intirely, for he hath redeem'd me, and is
even now sanctifying me with his own precious blood!—this day the sacrifice
was completed, "and he cried, it is finish'd" and bow'd his head, and yielded up
the ghost."—yea Jesus, the spotless Lamb of God in whom was found no sin,
hath died for me, to redeem me from sin, and Death eternal, and is even now
pleading for me at the right hand of his Father!—he pleads the merits of his
blood which cleanseth from *all* sin, and through which alone we can be
justified!

Easter Sabbath

"The Lord is risen indeed."—he hath ascended [forth] above the heavens
to plead for me,—even for me, for one so low as me, whom the world counts
nothing!—he has ascended, and I trust may meet congenial spirits on "a shore of

better promise."—Oh, glorious privilege, thus to believe, and thus to hope!—
and *this* shall bear me up amidst *disappointment*, and every *adverse* [seen]
{....}Yea, it is very pleasant to me to think, that "There is One that Sticketh
closer than a Brother."

March 29

Have been through the divine favor, permited to send on my annual
payment of Five dollars to the Theological Seminary in Alexandria for the
Education of pious Young Men to the Ministry of the Episcopal Church.—may
this little sum thus cast every year into the treasury of the Lord, be bless'd, as
was of Old, the Widow's mite!

Thursday

Have received an affectionate Letter from One of the Ministers of my
Church, acknowledging the receipt of the Five Dollars, for this, praised be the
name of the Lord!—have also received two other Letters from Christian
Friends—The Lord is good!

April 9—

Have just come from hearing the Rev. Mr. [...] deliver a discourse,—I am
not so well pleased with the two last discourses he has delivered in this place, I
say *discourses*, of methinks they cannot be call'd *Sermons*,—I believe the Rev.
Mr.—to be a zealous good Christian, but surely he has lately adopted a mode of
speaking to the people that must be I much fear unprofitable to both Saint, and
sinner.—ah, why does he tell how Infidels think?—why does he tell of the
objections made to Christianity?—let him leave all these things behind,
Infidelity is a bubble, it will burst of itself, if the lovely plan of Salvation can be
impress'd.—I would have the preacher to preach straight forward the *Gospel* as
it is in Christ Jesus, and to let infidelity alone, not to tell poor dying sinners *how*
they *do* think, but try to convince them *how* they *ought* to think—preach to them
the everlasting Gospel, preach it "forth in the words of Truth, and soberness"—
let him take of the things of God, and inform their judgements whilst he melts
their hearts.—let him tell how justice must be satisfied, and how that to appease
it a Saviour bled—that so great was our Sins, none other attonement could
suffice,—so foul our stains of sin that nothing less than the blood of *a God* wash
them out.—a Saviour has been given, *he* has *died* that *we* may *live*!—for as
many as *believe on him*, shall *be saved through him*,—the attonement once
made, saves all who shall receive it,—Jesus the spotless Lamb of God has made

an expiation for the sins of all that shall look to him and live, he it is that covers all their sins, and reconciles them to the Father,—he bides them "God and *sin no more*.—so greatly have we sin'd, that none other attonement could have been received,—none other blood than the blood of the incarnate God, the well beloved Son of the Father, could save us!—oh, let the Preacher endeavour with the help of God, not only to inform the understandings of poor Sinners, but to melt their stony hearts!—let him point them to the brow of mount Calvary and shew them the wounds that Sin has made.—so may each one hate their sins that has made such precious blood to flow! and may they love the bleeding sacrifice—Yea, Jesus, the spotless Lamb of God, hath made the expiation—the *one great attonement!* —he himself hath paid the precious ransom, and laid us under an everlasting debt of Love !—let poor Sinners behold the Saviour's bleeding side, and seek Salvation there!

April 16

This day we have again resumed our Sabbath school in this place which has been for some little time suspended,—may our Labours be bless'd in the Lord!

April 24

Have been for some days much indisposed.—a bad cold with much oppression on the Lungs.—could not go out yesterday to perform my duties at the Sabbath school.—nor attend the preaching of Mr.—have been told that he delivered an excellent Sermon, much better than the two last discourses I have heard form him.—I still hope, and still pray, that the {....} Lord may be pleased to bless him as the means of grace to this poor little desolate village of Port Royal.

May 2

Attended yesterday the Burial of another inhabitant of this apparently ill-fated village.—alas, the dispensations of divine Providence hanging over this unhealthy Spot are truly awful!—Poor old Man, thou art gone, and the place that once knew thee, shall know thee no more forever.—thy hoary head now rests beneath the clay.—cold sod of the Valley.—but whither, ah whither has the fleeting spirit fled?—awful consideration!

The Rev. Mr. Willer perform'd the Burial Service, and spoke feelingly and *well*, from the Seventh Chapter of Ecclesiastes.—methought I felt that it was good for me to be there, and that "it is better to go to the house of mourning, than to go to the house of feasting."—Lord let thy spirit so dwell in my heart that every lurking in may be banish'd from it, let me find on each day's examination, that I am thine, and enable me by thy grace not only to be ready to meet thee, but joyful to hail, and obey they summons, whenever thou shalt send thy messenger to call me home!—for why should I wish to tarry here? *a lonely, and a weary pilgrim in a vale of tears!*

May 8
Heard the Rev. Mr. Willer preach yesterday, and attended his Bible Class.

May 22
Heard the Rev. Presbyterian, preach yesterday from the 5th Chapt. of the second Epistle to the Corinthians 20th Verse—"Now then we are embassadors for Christ." etc.—it was such a sermon, as must have pleased all Christians, and I thought we had a delightful meeting, and that I did not come empty away.— One of the Baptist Brethren preach'd to us in the evening, I like very well what he said.

May 29
Attended as usual the Sabbath School on the morning of yesterday.—was prevented from going out in the evening to public worship by a severe Rain, and an oppression on my Lungs.—What needy, dependant creatures are we!—Oh, my Father, and my God, humbled at the foot of the Cross, I behold thy power, and confess my need of thee! then "direct me O Lord," in all my doings, with thy most gracious favour, and further me with thy continual help."—so may I be kept thine forever.

June 5
Heard yesterday a good Sermon from the Rev. Mr. Willer, he preach'd from the Beatitudes in the Saviour's Sermon on the Mount.—Let me not forget to note down a remarkable interposition of Providence which occur'd three days since—early on the morning of the second inst[...] going up Stairs, and in the act of raising one of the Windows, I appear'd to have step'd on somewhat that had an uncommon feel, soft, and roling under one of my feet,—I shriek'd and shudder'd, when I found that a Snake had subtley crept into the house, and coil'd itself just under the window that I had unwarily approach'd, and that my foot was even then on an enraged Serpent, that had its mouth open, and wreathed itself in passion,—my Woman had gone to the spring, there was no

human being in the house, but myself, and as I had just risen, I had carelessly slip'd my shoes on, without pulling them up at heel, and yet the Snake was not permited to hurt me—He who taketh account of even a Sparrow, at that moment took account of me, and prevented the bite of the Serpent.—it was a Snake of a dangerous kind.—I will often think of this interposition of divine providence in my favor—Yea, there is One who taketh account of the lone one, in her secret chambers,—then let me remember that he is with me, around me, and every where near.—and O, may I claim his very precious promise, that he will never leave me, or forsake me!—"There is One that sticketh closer than a Brother."

—Let me not say I am all alone! what though no *visible* objects are around me to love, yet is there not *One* whom *Unseen* I love, and who I trust loves me? for "he tempereth the wind to the shorn Lamb."—Even now, methinks some unseen spirit hovers near, and whispering says,

> "Each flattering hope, each anxious fear
> Each lonely sigh, each silent tear,
> To thine almighty friend is known
> And say'st thou, thou [...] all alone."

June 8

Much oppression on my lungs,—my cough increased.—Oh my heavenly Father, strengthen me with the comforts of thy holy spirit, Oh may I have an abiding sense of thy presence, and say alway thy name be praised, and under every dispensation of thy Providence. "Thy will and *not mine* be done!"—so may I be not only prepared, but joyfuly, and triumphantly welcome thy messenger that shall come to call me home!

June 13

The Methodists have had their Quarterly meeting here, it lasted three days, beginning one Saturday morning and ending last night.—The spirit seem'd to be abroad, striking conviction to the hearts of Sinners.—The meeting was very animated, and I hope Good was done in the name of the blessed Redeemer.—On the Sabbath, the Sacrament of the Lord's Supper was administer'd and I was glad to make one of those who surrounded the Table. for I love to avail myself of every opportunity of publicly acknowledging my Lord and Saviour.

I think my left Lung must be much diseased, from the feelings on my left side.—well, it may be, that my heavenly Father is about to call me home.—"Death is the Servant Jesus sends, to call us to his arms."—And will my blessed

Lord vouchsafe to own *me*, all unworthy as I feel myself?—he will not own me for any righteousness that *I* have done, for I am of myself *nothing*, but O, that blessed wedding Garment! clothed upon by *his* righteousness, and array'd in his own spotless robe, and the gates of Heaven will be open to receive me.—Jesus my all!—"An angel's arm can't snatch me from the grave, Legions of angels can't confine me there." Glorious thought!

July 10

Weak and indisposed in body, I yet went out yesterday Evening to hear the preached word.—The Rev. Mr. Vinton of the Methodist Church, preach'd from these words, "Give an account of the Stewardship, that thou may'st be no longer Steward."—an awful Text!—and well did the Methodist Brother, preach from it.—Oh, for that joyful Salutation,—Come ye blessed of my Father. etc!"—Yet a little while and I may be call'd to give an account of my Stewardship—Oh thou divine, and ever blessed Redeemer,—my Saviour, my all! thou who did'st hang in bleeding agony on the Cross, to save me, and all who shall look to thee from their Sins.—Oh do thou Remember Me!—

I have been thinking that the last verse of the Sixth Chapter of Romans, would be a good subject for a Burial Sermon,—"For the wages of Sin is death, but the gift of God is eternal life through Jesus Christ Our Lord.

Saturday Morn

By permission of divine Providence have been gratify'd in my wish of visiting Fredericksburg once again.—health still bad.—the Lord's will be done in all things!

Sabbath Morn

Have had the privilege of attending this day the worship of my own Church.—felt deeply impress'd by the solemn truths delivered By the Rev. Mr. McGuire.—his Text the 11th Verse of the 14th Chap. of the Gospel of St. John—"Believe me that I am in the Father, etc..."—My great high Priest!— divine Mediator!—what should *I* be, did I not believe on thee with all my powers?—yea, *I do* believe thee "for the very work's sake." and O divine, and adorable Redeemer, do thou remember me!—in the last conflict, when I shall have to encounter the last enemy, do thou remember me!—give me Victory over Death, and the Grave, then receive me to where thou art, to dwell forever with thee, and behold thy face without a veil between,—O, remember me in thy

Father's kingdom!—thy own words are, "In my Father's house are many mansions."—Lord remember me.

September 10

Return'd again to my dreary home in Port Royal, in wretched health of body.—no friend near me, none to sooth and sympathise.—no Friend on Earth!—but O, I hope and trust I have a Friend, yea, a Father in Heaven!—Father I stretch mine arms to thee, no other help have I, it is thou who art a friend of the friendless, and a Father of the Fatherless—it is thou, and *thou alone* O my heavenly Father who art my Friend, poor lonely weary pilgrim in a vale of tears!—but yet a very little while, and the days of my pilgrimage will be ended, disease with sure decay is making rapid progress on my frail, and amaciated frame.—Death, the messenger Death, will soon come and call me home.—O, my Father take home thy Child!

November 1

An extreme langour, and weariness from bad health has caused me to neglect even my favorite amusement of noting down my feelings, and the occurrences of the day, as time fleets away,—but though I have fail'd to write, yet has my mind not been inactive, I have *thought* much.—much about the things of time and sense,—and much, very much, about the weightier concerns of vast Eternity.—ah how much does the latter preponderate in the scale!—methinks I shall not much longer have to do with time and sense,—some persons are advising me to remove from this place, and yet boarded in some family, that it might perhaps be the means of improving my health, but I seem to dislike the thoughts now of making the exertion that such a removal would require, and yet if I thought that it was the will of the Lord, if I could once think that he call'd me to leave the Village, and my neat and rural habitation in it, I would go out in faith nothing doubting, for to do what I in my weak, and fallible judgement, think is the will of the Lord, is now my only wish.—it matters not with me now where I yield up this fleeting breath so that my Saviour's arms are around me.—Lord direct me by thy holy Spirit, the few remaining days of my pilgrimage, and then where soul, and body part,—oh then receive me up into glory!

November 10

I seem to think it is not the will of the Lord for me to quit my residence in Port Royal, for I know of no place at this time where I could get boarded and

believing it his will I am content to remain here, and have even made some
exertion to get the necessary comforts for the approach of Winter.—to do thy
will, O my God, is all my pleasure!

November 22

The ways of the Lord are past finding out! just when I thought it his will
that I should remain in Port Royal, lo, letters have arrived from my Sister in
Fredericksburg advising me, and beseeching me to remove from my lonely
abode and go and board with her, these Letters accompanied too, by messages
from my Mother saying that I must immediately remove.—my mind is
exercised, Lord direct thy tired, Suffering Child!

November 24

Have been much engaged in prayer I think the Lord from some of his
dealings, calls me to remove—it will be a great sacrifice of property my selling
out at this time, yet nevertheless the sacrifice shall be made, hoping as I do, that
I shall make it unto the Lord: my neat and rural dwelling, where I have
sometimes experienced good, and sometimes evil, where I have sometimes
experienced painful emotions, and where I have sometimes reposed and dreampt
of happiness, must be sacrificed,—yea, I have determined to part with it, with all
its beautiful growth of Roses, and Jessamine, and violets, and all its lovely
flowers, which I have nurtured with such care.—I give up all these, may it be for
good!

November 27

I have sacrificed my property,—Lord may I not be mistaken in supposing
that thou hast call'd me away! —soon the Hack will be down to bear me away to
Fredericksburg I feel now that there are some persons in it who I sigh to leave,
perhaps forever!—Lord may it be that I have not been mistaken, that I have been
directed by the councel, O may my removal be for good!

December 4

Arrived in Fredericksburg on Thursday, was well enough to attend the
Episcopal Church yesterday and heard an excellent discourse form him whom I
now consider as my pastor, the Rev. Mr. McGuire, his Text was from the last
Chapt. of Hebrews, eighth Verse.—"Jesus Christ the same yesterday, and to day,
and forever."—Praised be the Lord that I was well enough, to go out and hear

this Sermon! Lord thou knowest that I love thy sanctuary, and the place where thine honor dwelleth!

Sunday Morn

Though poorly in health, have been again permitted with the divine blessing, to attend worship in my own Church, heard a good sermon from the seventh Chapt. of St. John. 17 Verse.—Mr McGuire, has given notice that on the Sabbath he will administer the Sacrament of the Lord's Supper.—Oh my heavenly Father, if it seemeth good in thy sight, thine handmaid would pray to be enabled to attend on that day, and again renew her covenant with thee!— again acknowledge my Crucified but now risen Saviour in receiving the last memorials of his dying love.—and oh, let me remember that his blood was shed for me, and let me feed on him in my heart!—{....}

December 25

Hail, all hail, auspicious day, which brought a Saviour into the world,— blessed, forever blessed, the memorable day on which a God vouchsafed to visit earth, and condescend to take on himself our flesh, and to come even as a little Babe!—and what shall I render to thee my God for all thy benefits?—on this day the nativity of a Saviour, I am again permitted to raise my aspiring Soul to thee, to approach thee at a throne of grace, and supplicate a blessing from thee— yea, Lord bless me, even me, the least of all thy Servants, with an encrease of thy love,—and oh let the covenant I yesterday made with thee at thy own hallow'd board be more binding on me than ever, for I have again tasted the hallow'd bread, and drank of the sacred cup, the pledge, and token of a Saviour's Love,—I have been permitted the high privilege of receiving even from a Minister of my Own Church the consecrated elements—oh my God what shall I render to thee, who hast taken account of one even so low as me—I give myself to thee, 'tis all that I can do.—accept me Lord in all my feeble attempts to glorify thee, and at the last receive me up into glory!—Mr McGuire preach'd yesterday from the Lamentations of Jeremiah,—"Let us lift up our heart with our hands unto the Lord." and a most appropriate Sermon it was! well worthy of being remember'd by all who heard it, and more particularly by communicants.—today I hope again to tread the sanctuary of my God, O, may his spirit fill my heart, so may I profit by these high these estimated privileges!—in my weak, and feverish state of health, surely I may esteem it the gracious dealings of my heavenly Father that I am permitted sufficient strength of body to go out and hear the preached word.

Have return'd from hearing Mr. McGuire, give a delightful discourse
from the 2 Chapt. of St. Luke, 11 verse. "For unto you this day is born, etc."—I
praise, and thank the Lord, that I have bene permited to partake of the privileges
of my Church.—O may I when call'd away, rise from the Church Militant on
earth, to the Church triumphant in the Skies!

• 1827 •

February 8th, 1827 [82]

O, my heavenly Father, must thy tried, and tempted Child be still to the last, the sport of adverse gales?—but it is well,—perhaps there are some rebellious children that require to be lash'd to heaven by the scourge of adversity, who would otherwise never reach that happy place.—but it will soon all be over, yet a little while and I hope, and trust, I shall arrive at my Father's house, where his ever adorable son hath said there are many mansions.—oh that I may be admited to even the lowest seat!—bless'd, supremely bless'd, to dwell forever there, and unite with all the heavenly host in singing the wonders of redeeming love!—surely this cough, with the affection of my Lungs, tell me that I cannot much longer be a probationor in this Vale of tears.—O, my Father, take home thy Child!

March 5

Still, still I linger here!—ere this I had thought my spirit would have wing'd its flight to another, and I had hoped a better sphere,—and can it be presumption in me to hope that when this active spirit shall quit its frail tenement of clay, it shall wing its way on bouyant wing, to him who gave it being, and dwell forever with him through countless ages of eternal happiness?—can it be presumption when such a mighty ransom has been be paid, even the price of blood?—imperfect in myself, I look to one who has paid for me the debt.—the mighty victim has been slain! and through *him*, the all attoning sacrifice, I can lift an unpresumptious eye to heaven, and dare to hope for an unfading crown, even "a crown of life."—Jesus has died of me!—"my anchor hope shall safe abide," for it rests upon the rock of ages.—methinks I hear a voice proclaim.—"I am the resurrection and the life, he that believeth in me, tho he were dead, yet shall he live: and whosoever liveth and believeth in me, shall never die."—"Lord I believe, help thou mine unbelief."

Had the privilege of going to Church in the morning, of yesterday, and also in the evening, praised be the Lord for this!—Mr. McGuire, preach'd in the morning from the 6th Chapt. of St. Matthew, 33 verse,—and in the evening from the 61 Psalm.—I delight much in the truly gospel preaching of the Rev. Mr. McGuire.—One of his texts a few Sabbaths back, I forgot to note down.—

---

[82]The year is included with this date, since it is the first entry in 1827.

"For Christ is the end of the law for righteousness to every one that believeth."
Romans 10 verse 4—

March 11

Heard Mr. M. preach in the morning of yesterday, from the tenth Chapt. of Luke, part of the 42 verse. "But one thing is needful."—whilst he preach'd the truth, I could not forbear examining myself, and felt in how many instances of my Life I had greatly err'd in thinking too much of the things of Time, and Sense, and like Martha caring about many things, I felt that yet a little while, and I should have to give in my account.—O, my blessed Saviour, be thou my kind intercessor, and sheild me from the wrath of the Father!—may every day encrease my Faith and love, and now that the things of time and sense are fading on my view, may I every day feel more, and more, that my affections are placed above, and that like Mary I have chosen "the one thing needful."—Mr. M preach'd in the evening from the third Chapt. of Colossians.—third verse.—and it appear'd a delightful continuation of the discourse in the morning—Lord I thank thee that for two successive Sabbaths I have been enable to go out twice and hear thy preached word!—praise be thy holy name forever!

March 26

Went out twice to Church yesterday notwithstanding much bodily indisposition. Heard Mr. M preach in the Morning from Luke 22 Chapt. 61-62—Verse.—"And the Lord turned, and look upon Peter." etc.—and in the evening the text was from the 7th Psalm 11 verse—God judgeth the righteous." etc.—Oh, heavenly Father, let thy spirit be on me, so may I by every good sermon that I hear be profited to my soul's eternal welfare, and daily progress in Christian attainments.—and though thy hand bears heavy on me, yet let me not despise a Father's chastening rod.—hoping that these light afflictions are but for a moment and that they are preparing me for a better, and a more enduring kingdom.—yea,—perhaps the time is now near at hand, when I shall be landed on that world of spirits, from whence no traveler returneth.—O, for that shore of better promise, where the happy soul disencumber'd by the earthly tenement, become etherialized, and pure, uniting in the wisdom of the serpent, with the dove-like simplicity of the Child!

April 3

Could not attend Church yesterday morning, from bodily indisposition, and the dampness of the weather, but praised by the Lord, I was enabled to go out in the evening heard Mr. M lecture from the 63rd Psalm,—I had felt dull, and spiritless for some days, and a great deadness to spiritual things, I seem'd to have too little faith, too little love, but while in the sanctuary a better frame of mind appear'd to be accorded me, and methought I I found it was good for me to be there.—I felt great joy, and peace, in adopting the words of the royal psalmist.—"O God, thou art my God."—

April 9

Have been enabled with the help of God, to make my annual contribution this month for the Education of pious Young men to the Church and this notwithstanding all my loss's and cross's—oh that grace may be given to help me in every time of need.—Lord help me when I call upon thee, and bring me to hy kingdom, far from sin, and sorrow, where every tear is dried.—Attended Church twice yesterday—Mr. M. address'd himself in the morning to Parents and preach'd from this text—"Bring them up in the nurture, and fear of the Lord."—and in the evening he lectured on the subject of Prayer.

Good Friday

Jesus the immaculate Lamb of God has shed his sacred blood to cleanse me from all sins,—he hath wash'd me, he hath redeem'd me, and oh let me adore him!—in every situation let me remember my crucified Redeemer, his many afflictions, from his cradle in the manger, to his Cross on Mount Calvary. And whilst I remember his meek, and quiet spirit, let me learn to bear, and glory in the Cross of Christ,—and oh my God let thy spirit descend to strengthen me, so that I may always be enabled to say, Jesus hath died for me!

"Let sin no more my soul enslave,
Break , Lord, its tyrant chain,
O, save me whom thou camest to save
Nor bleed, nor die in vain!— "

Have just return'd from Church, heard Mr. M preach from St. John, 15 Chapt. 13 verse.—"Greater love hath no man,"—it was an excellent sermon.—Next Sabbath being Easter day, we shall have communion in the church.—my God make me more thankful, and encrease my faith, encrease my Love.

Sabbath Morn

Prevented by Rain from attending Church. This causes me to feel very heavy, and sorrowful, but it may be that the Lord sees fit to humble me, yea even in the very dust.—"Christ died for our sins, and rose again for our justification"—Oh, my blessed Saviour wilt thou manifest thyself to me as thou didst to thy Apostles of old; on this the third day after thy crucifixion.—Rise Sun of righteousness, arise, with healing on thy wings, and drive these dark clouds from my mind.—so my I enraptured exclaim "Christ has risen indeed."— yea risen and "become the first fruits of them that slept."

Sabbath Eve

My God I thank thee that I have this day, by thy permission been enable to delight myself in thy Sanctuary! methinks my soul has acquired fresh strength and support, I seem to lean on the bosom of my Saviour nothing doubting, through faith I behold him, and hope pointing me to his bleeding side tells me he has died for me, that Love divine has bought my pardon.—shall I then for one moment doubt that Christ will not keep what he has so dearly bought, that he will not love me to the end?—yea, Lord I believe,—"help thou mine unbelief."—Mr. M.—preach'd in the morning of this day from the ninth Chapt. of St. Matthew 28 and 29 verses, and this evening from the 15 Chapt. of St. Matthew, beginning at the 22 verse and ending with the 28 verse.—he beautifuly discoursed on the subject of Faith, and methought it was preaching intirely calculated to reassure me.—in faith I beheld the benevolent countenance of the Saviour of sinners, when at length he answer'd—"O woman great is thy faith: be it unto thee even as thou wilt."

Thursday Morn

On this day three Weeks hince, the Episcopal Convention will set in this Town.—I anticipate much satisfaction (if I am spared, and my health will permit) in attending at that time the preaching of my Ministers.—my God, let thy spirit be on the Preachers, and on the hearers of thy word, so may we all, both Saints and Sinners, be profited in listening to the eloquent strains of piety proceeding from the bright, and united lights of the Church—Oh my Father, may I be strengthen'd and feel my assurances brighten'd, by all I shall then hear! and may much good be done, in the holy name of the ever blessed Lord Jesus!— O it would be a goodly sight to behold poor sinners flocking to the blood stain'd banner, throwing down their arms of rebellion, and seeking their refuge at the foot of the Cross, where alone can be found the ark of safety!—it will be a joyful thing should it be hereafter said that it was good that the Episcopal convention set in Fredericksburg!

Monday Morn

Heard Mr. M.—preach yesterday from the 21st verse of the 50th Psalm.—
"These things hast thou done etc."

Sabbath Eve

Attended Church, morning and Evening.—Heard Mr. McGuire preach
from the first Book of Kings, 18 Chapt. 21 vers.—"How long halt, etc., etc."—
and in the evening from Exodus 33—15 verse.—"if thy presence etc."—Lord in
a few days there will be a meeting of many people, thine own people will
convene together in this place,—may it be for good,—O for the outpouring of
thy spirit as on the day of Pentecost!—wilt thou touch as with a coal the tongue
of thy own Embassadors, so may they preach thy words, and not their own, and
with more than angel's eloquence plead Immanuel's cause, and proclaim the
glad tidings of salvation.—Lord let me thy poor unworthy creature go to hear,
let me with thy help go up to thy Sanctuary feeling my need of the [...] like Mary
set at the feet of Jesus, choosing that good part which shall not be taken away.—
let thy spirit go with me for "if thy presence go not with me" it were better for
me I should not go up.—Lord meet us in thy sanctuary, and let thy presence be
us, and thy glory manifested to us as it was to Moses of old, so may we find rest
for our souls—

May 22

Lord I thank thee!—thou hast dealt graciously with thy people; we have
had a glorious convention and I think I may say a delightful season of refreshing
grace.—what multitudes [...] thronging the gates of Zion and some mourning
their sins, and longing the way to know Lord give to these mourners the oil of
gladness, for the sack cloth of ashes, and let thine own people still be
strengthen'd and supported by daily renewals of thy grace so may we go on our
way rejoicing, and thy Zion rear her drooping head—Heard many delightful
texts preach'd on with much energy and appropriate eloquence, but not being
acquainted with the different faces of the preachers, I cannot note down with
accuracy to whom the different sermons belong—but one [...] remarkable I will
not forget to note.—The Rev. Mr. Mead[83] exhorted at one of the prayer
meetings from a line, the first line of the second stanza of the thirtieth Hymn,
"Come Saints and drop a tear or two" this line he condemn'd, he thought a tear
or two, too trifling a tribute, when an enspired writer had said, "O that my tears

---

[83]Here, she is probably referring to Bishop Meade.

were rivers." etc.—the criticism on the line was just and the exhortation excellent, I have been attempting to alter the stanza, and have made it to run thus.

> Saints of the Lord your tears renew
> For him who groan'd beneath your load;
> Thousands of drops he shed for you,
> Rich drops of his own sacred blood.

Monday Morn

Was too much indisposed yesterday morning to go out to Church, went out in the evening, heard Mr. McGuire preach an excellent sermon from the sixth Chapt. of the gospel of St. John, 27 verse. "Labour not ye."—feel myself much indisposed.

June 12

Heard Mr. M preach yesterday from the 15 Chapter of the Gospel of St. John 22 Verse,—"If I had not come, etc" this text seem'd to remind me of my responsibility now that I have so many gospel privileges, may the Lord enable me to profit by every good sermon that I hear .—Heard Mr. M in the evening from the 19 chapt. of St. John part of 14 verse "Behold your King."—and Let us behold him crucify'd, and suffering for our sakes, and oh let us never again join with the unbelieving Jews, and crucify afresh the Lord of glory.—if sinners by their evil deed continue to cry crucify him crucify him, let us at least who have taken on us his sacred name, prove our allegiance by that "faith which works by love."—yea, let us "Behold our King." and enraptured cry, crown him, crown him, Lord of life, and glory!

Monday Morn

Heard Mr. M preach faithfully the Gospel yesterday morning, and again in the evening.—in the morning he preach'd from the 5th Chapter of Galatians, 1st verse "Stand fast etc."—and in the evening from the second epistle to the Corinthians, 3rd Chapt. 17th Verse.—"where the Spirit of the Lord is, there is liberty."—Oh glorious liberty, how much more desirable than the bondage of sin!—may I stand fast in the liberty wherewith Christ hath made us free."—felt much indisposed in body, yesterday, and today but praised be the Lord that I was able (notwithstanding this) to go to {...} I was shut out from all but *thee*, and when taking my bible have pray'd before thee and felt the blessed influences of the spirit assuring me that all my sins were cover'd—smile on me now, when most I need thy smiles, so may I find comfort and safety under thy sheltering wing amidst a stormy sea.—safe, though billows roar.—yea Lord manifest thyself to me, drive these dark clouds from my mind, and fill me with they perfect love.—thou knowest that when all alone, retired apart, unseen by all but thee, that it is my chief delight to pour forth my soul before thee, and to think with sweet comfort and peace of thee my God in solitude.—then come to me, O thou whom my soul lovest—my company, my comforter, my only friend!—yet a little while, and time shall give place to eternity, then shall appear that heaven of love, and everlasting joy where in dwelleth righteousness, and where in no wise shall enter any thing that defileth, but all shall be one bright scene of glory, and love, and harmony!—then shall I be ever with O, my God! thou blessed Spirit, divine Sanctifier!—Jesus my life my all!—Shall [dwell] with thee without a veil between!

(Judith Lomax died on January 19, 1828)

• Poetry and Fragments •

A Sacramental Effusion[84]

And dost thou now great God prepare
Thine honor'd banquet from above;
And tho' a sinner may I dare,
To share again that feast of Love

With trembling awe I thus presume,
and feel alas the weight of sin,
Feel that thou only can'st illume,
My mind, and make it pure within.

Then whilst each penitential tear,
Bears witness to a contrite heart;
Let thy rich comforts banish fear,
And Love, and Joy and Peace impart.

And of thy Cup, while thus I taste,
And eat of Life, the Sacred Bread;
O, let thy quick'ning spirit haste,
and o'er me all its influence shed.

So may I to my Father's board,
approach, and claim a pardon free;
Say, blessed be his name ador'd
A Saviour's blood hath ransom'd me!

And, Lord of Life! to all around,
who now have to thy Table prest;
Let still thy Love, and Peace abound,
so may thy means of grace be blest!

And let the blessing widely spread
Till countless numbers throng thy board;

---

[84]At this point the original manuscript consists of a series of pages of poetry.

till *all* shall share their Father's bread,
till *all* shall own him Sov'reign Lord!

An Elegeac Tribute to the Memory Of My Beloved Christian Friend, Mrs. Jane Jett

And is she gone who lately shone
    In Christian lustre bright?
Yes, heav'n sees good to call its own,
    to realms of endless Light.

Her Soul became too pure for earth.
    when sanctified by grace;
And having known a second birth,
    soon sought its native place.

Why mourn the Sainted friend at rest,
    since Death ensures her peace?
since Death is but the herald blest,
    That bids each sorrow cease?

Then sigh not winds as softly o'er,
    Her newmade grave ye fly,
Weep not ye dews!—on earth no more,
    will she e'er weep or sign.

O, now, in brighter scenes she wakes,
    With wreaths of glory crown'd!
and with a holy band partakes,
    The streams which there abound.

For tho mouldering with the dead,
    And low the Body lies;
Yet sure, the Sainted soul has fled
    Up to its native skies!

Then sign not winds as softly o'er,
Her new made grave ye fly;
Weep not ye dews!—on earth no more,
will she e'er weep or sigh!

Devotional Stanzas

Thou God of Truth! who rul'st above,
O, sanctify this heart of mine;
Make it the temple of thy love,
Thus sealing it forever thine!

How sweet the bond that love shall bind!
How sweet to be the child of Heav'n!
A Father's tender care to find
His saving grace the treasure giv'n!

Giv'n to know the blood that flow'd,
In purple streams on Calvary;
Flow'd not in vain, but hath bestow'd,
Redemption on poor rebel me.

Yes, yes, I feel the vital force,
Of those rich streams that cleanse the heart
They flow with purifying course,
Before them all my doubts depart.

For if in Christ I do believe,
If him I love, then I am sav'd
God's holy word can ne'er deceive,
That giv'n, is on my heart engrav'd.

And O, that word unchang'd shall prove
When Earth, Seas, World shall pass away
That Word—His Truth—His wond'rous Love
'Tis these alone shall not decay.

And these thro' Faith my heart assure
That sins unnumber'd are forgiv'n;
These make my happiness secure,
And plant my hope, my joy *in Heav'n*.

Let persecutions, or distress,
Or ev'ry earth-born care annoy;
They ne'er can make my comforts less,
If I the love of Christ enjoy.

How sweet the bond which thus can bind!
How sweet to be the Child of Heav'n!
A Father's tender care to find
His saving grace the treasure giv'n!

For tho' the Dead make no report,
We know of *one* who did arise;
Ascending to his Father's Court,
To plead for us above the skies.

And now he comes in Royal state,
Hark!—hear again the Trumpet sound!
A Saviour comes!—and Angels wait,
While Judgement awful, peals around.

Behold the Saviour of the World!
His shining Robes in air they stream,
His banner now is all unfurl'd,
And bright around his glories beam.

So now! the Grave, it cannot keep,
The light and disembodied Soul;
For active, that can never sleep,
No grassy mound, can it control.

Bursting its fetters 'twill be free,
And ruin'd sink, or rise to joy;

It *must be judg'd*! 'its his decree,
Whose mandate nought can e'er destroy.

The summon'd Spirit now must stand,
Whether the prize be lost, or won;
And give account at God's command,
Of deeds that in the flesh were done.

And woe, to those who never sought
His saving grace while yet they might!
For *such* no ransom has been bought,
Yet awe-struck they *must* meet his sight.

How may they hear that sentence dire?
Go from my face!—accursed go!
Go into everlasting Fire,
And meet thy never ending woe!

But, the good Shepherd knows his Sheep,
The willing ones who heard his voice;
And faithful he has been to keep,
The little flock of his own choice.

Chosen, because they still would dare,
To count for him all else but loss;
And these it is the crown shall wear,
For they have borne their Master's cross.—

Now comes a Voice! it softer floats,
Then breezes on the silken string;
When Angels seem to strike the notes,
And make around sweet musick ring.—

Come blessed of my Father, come!
For there are many mansions here;
Come rest in this thy happy home,
Thou who hast been his tender care.

Here, with the co-eternal Three,
While yet Eternity goes round;
Thy joys shall still successive be,
For thou art good and faithful found.

Join now that lovely host above,
Bearing their palms, in white they stand;
And all surround the Throne of Love,
A beautiful, and holy band!

'Mongst them, some Herald once of peace,
Who ere he reach'd his Father's home,
Had warn'd thee from thy sins to cease,
And now he joys to see thee come.

Here meet again that Christian Friend,
Meet him in Christ to part no more;
Where pleasures centre without end,
Where sin, and sorrow, Tears are o'er.

Yet would thy joys imperfect run,
Even amidst that Sainted host;
Without the Spirit *Three in One*,
The *Father, Son and Holy Ghost*.

This presence tis that shines above,
And makes a place of heav'nly rest;
Kindling the flame of Sainted Love,
In each enraptur'd, glowing breast.

The Magdalene, [Luke...]

When the poor Female sinner sought,
The Saviour's sacred feet;
An Alabaster Box she brought;
With precious ointment sweet,

And still she wept, and stood behind,
Nor dared to meet his face;
For Sin too sore opprest that mind,
Which scarcely hoped for grace.

But at his feet, she threw her cares,
And pour'd the ointment there;
Then kiss'd, and wash'd them with her tears,
And wiped them with her hair,

'Twas then the Pharisee in pride,
Bethought him of her sin;
But Jesus bade her to confide,
Since all was *Love* within.

Her sins tho' many, were forgiv'n,
Then must her sorrows cease!—
Her Faith, and *Love*, the gain'd her Heav'n,
He bade her—go in peace.—

Love for the Saviour!—oh, how pure!
How sweet the sacred flame!
Since grace so rich, it could secure,
When she a sinner came,

Dear Lord! may I like her attone,
By penitence each sin;
That when I dare approach thy throne,
I may find peace within.

And since Heav'n's attribute's divine,
Are peace, and holy love;
Oh! let me strive to make these mine,
And seal my joys above.

May all of us from day, to day
In faith our God adore;
So may he bid us go our way,
[In peace] and sin [no more].

On the Happiness of this World

Worldly bliss! enchanting wound!
Thou pleasing, but delusive theme!
So often sought, but seldom found,
And but at best a splendid dream!

Oft dost thou mock the *rich*, the *gay*,
Who grasp at joys that swiftly fade;
And grandeur views thee melt away;
Thou dazzling but too empty shade!

Since then the world has nought to give,
but these too unsubstantial joys;
Oh let us seek those gifts that live,
Far beyond such glitt'ring toys.

For yet there is a hallow'd light,
That beameth o'er the spotless breast;
Where wisdom sheds her rich delight,
Where Virtue seeks her place of rest.

And in that bright ethereal mind,
True happiness alone is found;
'Tis there rich treasures are combined,
Which dwell not with the World around.—

Fragments

Often at the sight of a Lovely Country we are tempted to believe that its only object is to excite in us exalted an spotless admiration, but soon this sentiment becomes still more elevated, our feelings are by degrees spiritualized, and involuntarily our thoughts ascend to that omnipotent Creator whose works at that moment appear so wonderful and so lovely to our enraptured view— There is surely a delightful connection existing between the beautiful and sublime scenery of nature, and the human heart,—between the rays of the moon that repose on the adjacant hills, and the calm of conscience, between the opening flower that expands itself to meet the beams of the rising day, and the mind that opens to the reception of truth, seeking that heavenly light that divine wisdom, which God by the influences of his spirit is ever ready to impart.— [Be]hold a lovely language to the thinking mind, and there are times when we are capable of yielding wholly to the agitation they excite—this abandonment is good for the soul!—for when at eve we view the boundary of the landscape, and the heaven appears to recline so closely to the earth, the imagination then soars beyond this terrestrial sphere, (all lovely as it at that moment appears to us) and sketch's beyond the horizon a heaven of hope, a native land of love, and Nature! all nature! in silent, but affecting language proclaims to us the immortality of the Soul.—
We must be very ignorant of Christianity if we do not think it admits of the highest cultivation of the human mind,—I would have Religion appear as it is—lovely in every point of view!—Oh! let us open the gates of the temple, let us call to our support Genius, the fine arts and the sciences, let us assemble them in one [focus], to honor and to comprehend the Author of creation.—and it to the spiritual mind the God of Love, of Truth, of Wisdom appears emblazon'd throughout creation [...] extent, shall not this same Godhead appear in every thou[ght] [...] attaches itself to the [...]nal chain.

Fragments

We must possess imagination to make us conjecture all that the heart [can] cause us to suffer, there are some people, and the best sort of people too in the world, who are perhaps a little dull in this respect: they march right across our feelings, as if they were treading upon flowers and wondering that they fade away.—But "is there no balm in Gilead? is there no physician there?"—Yes, there is a sacred stream which when sought for, never fails to heal. There is a Physician able to

Cure, ev[...] Christ that great physician, and his streams the balm that never [...]—The almighty breath of Religion sheds o'er the feelings a heavenly peace that nothing earthly can dispel.—The sensate heart imbued by the influence of the holy spirit, turns,—trembling turns towards the pole it loves, and its feelings all sanctified and holy, seek a higher direction than this little clad of earth.—soaring to the God that purifies them!—it is then that those very feelings which have been the cause of pain, become sources of exquisite felicity, for they give us to experience that lively joy in God, which seems to be already a foretaste of Heaven—and tho we may sometimes be discouraged in our hopes, and almost fear that the Godhead is retiring, and hiding away his face,—yet we remain not less faithful to the sacred influence.—there *is* incense in the temple, there *is* music in the sanctuary, there *is* emotion in the heart, and it still turns trembling towards the pole it loves.—even to God, the great Physician.—

This Life has not value unless it is subservient to Religion, unless while here on Earth—by our freely accepting the offer'd influences of the Divine Spirit, which are I believe at one time or other offer'd to *all*, and thro which we are enabled to do the will of that great and invisible being, who created us that he might in his own good pleasure, and at his own good time, exalt us higher,—Then let us not refuse his offer'd bounty, his offer'd Salvation, purchased by the richest blood that ever flow'd!—Let us not be found out of the path of duty!—and with the grace of God, let us by a happy mixture of contemplation and of activity, of resignation, and of will connect our earthly existence with heaven!

–Sanctified by the holy spirit, let our every Thought, Word, and [Deed], be pure and holy.—thus shall we be prepared at the last, [for] that higher elevation of destiny which a[waits] us!—even for the c[om]pany of beatified Spirits, and the pr[esence] of our God and Saviour! —

Index